Reading Minds

Reading Minds

How Childhood Teaches Us to
Understand People

HENRY M. WELLMAN

WITH KAREN LIND

OXFORD
UNIVERSITY PRESS

Oxford University Press is a department of the University of Oxford. It furthers
the University's objective of excellence in research, scholarship, and education
by publishing worldwide. Oxford is a registered trade mark of Oxford University
Press in the UK and certain other countries.

Published in the United States of America by Oxford University Press
198 Madison Avenue, New York, NY 10016, United States of America.

CIP data is on file at the Library of Congress
ISBN 978–0–19–087867–2

1 3 5 7 9 8 6 4 2

Printed by Sheridan Books, Inc., United States of America

Contents

List of Sidebars

Preface

On March 5, 2007, NBCNews.com posted an article, "Mindreading Scientists Predict Behavior."[1] It began, "At a laboratory in Germany, volunteers slide into a donut-shaped MRI machine and perform simple tasks, such as deciding whether to add or subtract two numbers." Scientists in the next room were trying to read these volunteers' minds—to judge what the persons intended in thought before they acted. They did this by examining the brain scans from the magnetic resonance imaging (MRI). The researchers, led by a Dr. Haynes in Berlin, were reasonably successful: They identified the subjects' decisions about what they would do, in this case adding versus subtracting, at a rate better than chance.

Participants were told to decide whether they would add or subtract two numbers a few seconds before any numbers were flashed on a screen. During those few seconds, the scanner provided computer-enhanced images of the participants' brain activity, and the researchers used those images to predict the subject's decision—with one brain pattern suggesting an intention to add and another an intention to subtract. As the story admitted, "The research, which began in July 2005, has been of limited scope: only 21 people have been tested so far. And the 71 percent accuracy rate is only about 20 percent more successful than random selection."

Still, reactions were strong:

"The fact that we can determine what intention a person is holding in their mind pushes the level of our understanding of subjective thought to a whole new level," said Dr. Paul Wolpe, a professor of psychiatry at the University of Pennsylvania.

Tanja Steinbach, an adult participant, said "It's really weird. But since I know they're only able to do this if they have certain machines, I'm not worried that everybody else on the street can read my mind."

Some commentators were alarmed by the implications of such mind reading. "Scientists are making enough progress to make ethicists nervous."

Reading minds—amazing.

Yet two- and three-year-olds do it every day, and even infants can figure out someone's intentions, as we'll see. Young children don't need fancy machines. Instead, they use their ordinary, still-developing cognitive abilities to detect and infer people's mental states: their states of mind. In fact, we all read minds in this mundane but nonetheless amazing way.

The writer of this article talks about the commentators' *enthusiasm* or *alarm*. A friend looks up at a clear, star-studded nighttime sky, and we see her *wonder*. The passenger next to us on the plane stands up in midflight and struggles to reach into the overhead bin, and we know he *intends* to get something from there. When he gets his laptop out, we understand, "That's what he *wanted*." That we all do this every day, that even children can do it, does not deny the power and the wizardry of this ordinary mind reading. And, we're often good at it: We can do it better than these scientists without using costly machinery. We're not infallible, but we're probably at least 70 percent correct for simple things like inferring intentions in constrained situations and using them to predict choices. And we read minds in far more complicated situations.

How do we do it? Why and when do we learn it, and how does this impact our lives, our sense of self, our actions and interactions with others? What happens if someone cannot do it? What happens when we're wrong? I answer all these questions in the course of the book. But, the short answer is that reading minds is the backbone and business of our lives.

I've been interested in these questions and answers for thirty years. So have a legion of other scientists. I owe them a lot. Names for some of them appear throughout the book, but without citations. Those appear in the Notes for each chapter. When I quote from others' writings or stories, for the sake of readability I have avoided elipses (. . .) and brackets, but I have tried valiantly to make sure that any omissions or abridgements have not changed the author's meaning. The Notes cite where the original, unabridged quotations can be found.

I owe a very large debt to these scientists as well to the strangers, parents, and children who have participated in our work.

Reading Minds

1

Reading Minds 101

In 2010, thirty-three Chilean miners were discovered alive seventeen days after being trapped below more than a mile of rock and dirt. Through a thin electric line threaded down to them, the miners were able to send messages to the top. One man's first message to his wife said

> We *thought* we were going to starve to death down here. You can't *imagine* how much my soul *hurt wanting* to tell you, but unable to let you *know* we were alive.[1]

This message radiates one of the most basic aspects of our humanity: We constantly think of others and ourselves in terms of our inner mental lives. In this harrowing situation, the stakes were high, and the miner's message contained little else. The miner *thought* he might starve. He *hurt* with his inability to communicate with his wife. He was distressed she hadn't *known* he was alive.

And almost surely, with your own well-developed ability to read and interpret mental states, you read between the lines of his message and added more. You sensed in his statement things like fear, determination, hope, and exhaustion. You don't know the miner's state of mind for certain, but you know he's been underground for seventeen days; you know he's finally been located and that rescue operations have begun. From his words and from that knowledge, you might well read relief as well as physical and emotional exhaustion into his words.

That you can do this is a definitive part of being human. All day, every day, we try to get into the minds of other people. We observe their words and actions to figure out their thoughts, feelings, hopes, and intentions. And amazingly, we can do it. We can penetrate into other people's inner mental states, and we can read, interpret, and communicate our own mental states— to explain ourselves to others and to clarify our thoughts for ourselves.

This everyday, ordinary mind reading is something we begin to learn in infancy, and by adulthood we do it incessantly. Without thinking about it,

Reading Minds. Henry M. Wellman with Karen Lind, Oxford University Press (2020) © Oxford University Press.
DOI: 10.1093/oso/9780190878672.001.0001

in myriad split-second assessments or in deeply considered judgments, we are all reading minds all the time. We can't help ourselves, and we wouldn't want to.

Reading minds is a vital human skill because humans are intrinsically social—even the most solitary of us lives socially. We are raised by parents, in families and communities, constantly interacting with, caring about, and working with other people. Not surprisingly, we want to make sense of this social world to understand ourselves and others. It brings order and predictability to human interactions that might otherwise seem frightening and painfully random.

Only humans so extensively develop this ability to read minds. Anthropologists theorize it was crucial to our evolution as *Homo sapiens*.[2] Indeed, this skill is so fundamental to human survival that researchers have found its beginnings in babies only ten or twelve months old. From that time, we grow increasingly skilled at, and increasingly dependent on, understanding our own and others' minds.

Reading minds is so ingrained a part of our lives that we can fail to notice how constantly we do it. A family sits around the dinner table on a Friday night. The raw perceptions that hit our eyes without the benefit of mind reading are

> Bags of skin stuffed into pieces of cloth and draped over chairs that move in unpredictable ways, with small restless black spots that move at the top of the bags and a hole underneath that irregularly makes noises.[3]

It's eerie and unfamiliar. But if we add some basic social understanding, the bags of skin become humans, the noises become: "Pass the potatoes." "What's for dessert?" Add mind reading, and we understand the father *wants* potatoes. The girl *prefers* dessert over vegetables. The boy fidgets, and we can almost hear him *thinking,* "Aren't we done yet?" We do this ordinary, powerful mind reading constantly as we try to work out the thoughts others hold. Psychologists call this our **theory of mind**.

Theory of mind sets us apart as human; it defines the way we think about ourselves and others. We are the only species that incessantly wonders and worries about what others are wondering, wanting, and worrying about.

Amazingly, this huge and diverse understanding is not spoon-fed to us or given in a script we can learn by rote. Each of us creates a wide-ranging theory of mind that we use to understand how all people work socially. We use this theory throughout our lives to read minds and to make sense of our social world. The focus of this book is how we develop this theory of mind as children and how that defines us as individuals and highlights us as human.

How We Begin

When my son, Trey,* had just turned four he once told me, "Shut your eyes."

"Why?" I asked.

"I'm going to do something you don't like."

Trey was beginning to read minds, but because he was so young, he got only partway there. He understood that concealment could help him get what he wanted: I wouldn't know, so I wouldn't object. But he didn't understand the next step: I needed to stay ignorant for his strategy to work.

We can watch these developmental fits and starts in any child. Parents watch children learn to crawl, then walk, then run. We watch them talk, then read and write. In the same way, researchers watch children learn to read minds. One-year-olds show theory-of-mind insights that develop and unfold, just like physical or language skills, throughout their childhood.

When Trey was nearly three, we ended a trip to the zoo with a stop at the gift shop. He was entranced by a display of puppets: penguins, baby lions, fuzzy snakes, and giraffes.

"I want one," he said.

"You have a birthday coming. You could get one for that," we told him.

Sure enough, on his birthday he opened a box with a lion cub in it—and burst into tears. Once he calmed down, he explained, "But, but, I want one that's green and furry."

Back at the shop he pointed to the green alligator. That alligator, promptly named "Boufie," and his successors (Boufie 2, Boufie 3, and Boufie 4) became members of our family. As did Boufie's wants, mouthed by Trey on Boufie's behalf.

Understanding and insisting on wants is one of the first steps along our theory-of-mind path. Almost all parents remember the terrible twos. It's a time when children first realize their wants are different from their parents' and they begin to insist, fiercely, vocally, on their own. It's how Boufie entered

---

* This is a made-up name. I have two sons; for their privacy, the events I attribute to Trey represent a mixture from both their lives.

our lives. If Trey had been twelve months old, he wouldn't have understood that he could have, and voice, wants different from ours.

Reading the Minds of Others

After knowing about their own and others' wants comes the step when a child can predict what people will think. In Trey's case, when he told me to hide my eyes, his thought was something like, "If Dad sees me, he'll know I'm doing something he's outlawed." We gave Trey a classic test that reveals this skill in my child laboratory at the University of Michigan. First, we showed him two boxes. One was a candy box; the other was plain white. When I asked him what was in the candy box, he said, "Candy!" But when he opened the box, he found it was empty. Instead, the plain box was full of candy.

I closed the boxes back up as Glenda, my research assistant, came in. "Glenda loves candy," I told him. Glenda nodded enthusiastically. "Where will Glenda look for candy?"

Trey first tried this task at age three-and-a-half and then again when he had just turned five. The change in his ability during that period was dramatic. At age three-and-a-half, Trey, along with almost all children that age, said Glenda would look for the candy in the plain box because he knew that's where the candy was.

At this age, children understand people can have different wants, hence the terrible twos. But, they often believe people all have the same thoughts. They know where the candy is, so, of course, Glenda also does. Not surprisingly, at this age children expect their parents to know where they put their shoes, what happened at preschool, and if they washed their hands, even if their parents weren't around when these things happened.

But five-year-old children? Eighty percent of them say Glenda will look in the candy box, just as Trey did on his second visit. With a year and a half of additional development, children can now separate Glenda's thinking from their own. They understand that if Glenda wants candy, she will look where *she* thinks it is, in a candy box. Her actions are driven by her incorrect beliefs, not by where the candy really is. Glenda has a false belief about where to find candy, and five-year-olds can follow her mental processes to predict this.

Smart? Absolutely. But this is an intelligence that virtually every child in every society on our planet develops. It's child's play, effortless. And easy as children find these steps to be, they are the basis of our singular human capacity to read minds. Forming a theory of mind is not a seamless effort, but its complex assembly shows us how we come to understand the workings of the human social mind. It is, in fact, the story of how we become human.

Without a theory of mind we couldn't cooperate or compete with others, understand ourselves, make friends, learn to lie and deceive and pretend, interact with robots and smartphones, and almost universally become gossips. It is basic to why some of us become religious believers and others atheists, why some of us become novelists and all of us love stories, why some love scary movies and some hate them.

Mistakes Are Made

Basic to understanding theory of mind is understanding that it is theory not fact. It provides your best interpretation of what's going on after filtering all your information through the lens of your current theory. And sometimes the lens is distorted and you come up with the wrong answer—either for yourself or for others. You can see this in four-year-old Adam, when he eats glue[4]:

ADAM: "I don't like it."
HIS MOTHER: "Then why would you put it in your mouth?"
ADAM: "I thought it was good."

Adam thought eating glue would give him a delicious treat. He finds out he's wrong; he held a false belief. His new thinking: If you want a treat, don't go to the glue jar.

Much of our early life is driven by our efforts to learn what we want and what we don't and to learn when our thoughts are correct and when they're false. At the same time, we're learning similar things about others. This is learning that continues throughout adulthood.

Take that fluffy, blue, mohair shawl you gave Aunt Lib. You chose the shawl because you thought it would please her. But it was clear from her face when she opened the gift that, hard as she tried to mask it, the gift failed. At this point, your theory of mind probably kicked in again. Why hadn't she liked it? Did she hate blue? Was she allergic to mohair? Did she think shawls were only for elderly women, and she didn't want to be one of them? You were searching for more theory-of-mind information to make better sense of Aunt Lib.

Aunt Lib getting a disappointing gift, Glenda not getting tasty candy, and Adam eating glue are unfortunate. But theory-of-mind fallibility can be the backbone of tragedy.

Romeo and Juliet, a story that has endured for centuries, is based on this kind of error. Its ending stems from a fatal false belief.

Because their families are intractable enemies, Romeo and Juliet marry secretly and then must escape the city and their warring relatives. Romeo has to flee immediately, but he will return to help Juliet escape. While he is gone, Juliet develops a plan. She takes a powerful drug to make her appear dead for a few days. She will wake after being interred in the family crypt, Romeo will meet her there, and then she and Romeo can escape together. But Romeo doesn't learn Juliet has taken the drug and finds her in the crypt, seemingly dead. In despair, not wanting to live without her, he poisons himself and dies. When Juliet awakes, and finds Romeo dead, she kills herself.

Their wrenching tragedy grows from Romeo's false belief, an error that adult playgoers have anguished over for centuries. But interestingly, when some of the play's complexities are shed, children as young as age five can understand that Romeo acts on a thought that is false. It is a step they have taken toward developing their own well-organized, incessantly employed, adult theory of mind.

Yet, a few people don't develop this theory of mind, and they teach us as much as children and Shakespeare do.

Life Without Reading Minds: Autism and Mindblindness

Temple Grandin is probably the most famous, and one of the most high-functioning, autistic adults in the world. Despite her intelligence and accomplishments—she is a professor of animal science at Colorado State University—Grandin, like individuals with autism in general, does not have our ordinary theory of mind. Far from being able to read minds, she has been called mindblind.[5]

Grandin, and others with autism, give us an idea of what it might be like to live without a theory of mind and without mind reading. In her own words, Grandin said she just doesn't "get" human socialization and interaction. She has had to try to learn it, piece by puzzling piece, as an outsider. "Much of the time," she told Oliver Sacks in a 1993 interview, "I feel like an anthropologist on Mars."[6]

In her conversations with Sacks, Grandin told of her early work designing and implementing her first humane cattle slaughterhouse. When the plant was first up and running, it had unending breakdowns in spite of her careful research and planning. Why?

Grandin tracked every possible physical factor to discover the cause. She eliminated one after another, until she realized the only constant was one worker, John. Only then did she consider that the world of livestock handling at that time was the province of men. As a woman, and as socially odd, she drew envy and suspicion. And that led to human malfeasance—a cause she had never considered. "I had to learn to be suspicious."

As Sacks wrote, "In her ingenuousness and gullibility, Temple was at first a target for all sorts of tricks and exploitations. She had a guilelessness arising from her failure to understand dissembling and pretense." Because of her autism, it didn't occur to her to look into the motivations of another person or to suspect that those motivations might be intended to thwart her. She also has said she is bewildered by *Romeo and Juliet*. She told Oliver Sacks, "I never knew what they were up to."

No two people with autism are the same, in personality, life history, or competence. Because of the wide range of symptoms and deficits, experts say these individuals fall on an autism spectrum. The most high-functioning autistic individuals can achieve normal or even above-normal levels of language and overall IQ. Individuals with autism develop, but their development is disordered.

This happened to Temple Grandin. At age three she had no language whatsoever, often a predictor of severe limits on future development. She was diagnosed with brain damage in her preschool years and slotted for institutionalization. But her mother refused to accept this and arranged private speech therapy and special, intensive school experiences for Temple. Slowly Grandin "emerged." Her 1986 autobiography is titled *Emergence: Labeled Autistic*. "Language just gradually came in, one or two words at a time. Before then, I would just scream. I couldn't talk." She is now a highly verbal, famous designer of livestock-handling facilities.*

---

* Grandin's official website says livestock facilities she has designed are located in the United States, Canada, Europe, Mexico, Australia, New Zealand, and other countries. In North America, almost half the cattle slaughtered are handled in a system she designed.

Grandin's level of achievement and accomplishment is unusual among individuals with autism, but it has not mitigated her severe and ongoing problems in understanding and interacting with others. The social world of people continues to perplex her. Only over years has Grandin learned, by brute force, some of the ways of the world that typically developing people understand effortlessly. She has developed some methods to compensate for her theory-of-mind deficits.

Uta Frith, an autism expert in England, wrote, "Autism does not go away. Autistic people can, and often do, compensate for their handicap to a remarkable degree. Yet there remains a persistent deficit, something that cannot be corrected or substituted." There is no cure and no "growing out of it."[7]

Grandin has said, "If I could snap my fingers and be non-autistic, I would not—because then I wouldn't be me." But she also has written poignantly about what she is missing:

> I do not fit in with the social life of my town or university. Almost all my social contacts are with livestock people or people interested in autism. Most of my Friday and Saturday nights are spent writing papers. My interests are factual and my recreational reading consists mostly of science and livestock publications. I have little interest in novels with their interpersonal relations.

She concludes, "My life would be horrible if I did not have my challenging career."

As Grandin proves, living without a theory of mind is possible. But she spotlights what happens when a person fails to develop the ordinary mind reading we use every day, as we work out what others are thinking, wanting, and feeling.

Going Forward

Theory of mind pervades all childhood development. It is more than, and much more intriguing than, how children (and babies, apes, and adults) perform one laboratory test or another. Acquiring everyday theory of mind is one of our species' most impressive intellectual accomplishments: a grand, foundational achievement. It becomes even more impressive when we see early understandings blossom into adult competencies or blind spots.

Reading Minds shows how ordinary children learn to read minds in a series of steps that are orderly, predictable, and fascinating. A failure to learn these steps cripples a child, and ultimately an adult, in areas as diverse as achieving social competence, creating a coherent life story, enjoying drama and movies, and living on one's own. An understanding of these steps allows us to see the nature of our shared humanity, to understand our children and our childhood selves, to teach and to learn from others, and to better navigate our social worlds.

In *Reading Minds* I trace the connection between a three-year-old's initial insights about pretending and how novelists create realities by making things up. I show how a six-year-old's understanding of superheroes leads to a theologian's conception of and relation with God and the afterlife. And I show how children's burgeoning awareness of internal feelings and thoughts is tied not only to the terrible twos, but also to their spontaneous sympathy for distress, which in turn leads to our adult moral and legal reasoning.

In doing this, *Reading Minds* introduces you to liars, scientists, cute children, different cultures, ordinary and extraordinary minds, and the workings of babies, brains, chimps, and dogs. It shows you how children rely on their ever-expanding theory of mind to develop into politicians, scientists, teammates, and conmen.

Reading Minds addresses questions about our social world whose answers spring from our childhood mindreading. Why are we fascinated with gossip? Why do we talk with each other, and even our pets and appliances? Why are our media, our children's books, and our self-understandings so saturated in stories? What about the afterlife, imaginary companions, faith in deities, personal identity, or omniscience?

I have never met a person who is not curious about people. *Reading Minds* helps satisfy that curiosity.

2

Mind Reading, Gossip, and Liars

Adults, in all societies and cultures, love to gossip. Gossip takes up about 65 percent of our speaking time, according to researchers who have listened to conversations in shopping malls, subway cars, and airport lounges.[1] And this holds true no matter the age or the gender of the speaker.

There are exceptions of course. Temple Grandin has written that social chitchat bores her. As a teen, her peers' interactions seemed pointless; the girls talked about clothes, boyfriends, and what X said to Y. "I could not understand why my peers spent hours talking about some topic with no real substance."[2]

For the rest of us, gossip is endlessly fascinating—to the point that scientists have wondered why.

Gossip: Can You Blame Your Primate DNA?

In his book *Grooming, Gossip, and the Evolution of Language*, comparative anthropologist Robin Dunbar argued that gossip has its roots in our primate heritage, and that humans are the primate that excels at it.

Gossip is often discounted; it's said to be untrue or unsupported, dishing dirt. But gossip, in essence, is any revealing account about another person—good or bad, true or false. And gossip appeals to us in part because it gives us a massive arena for learning about the inner workings of far more people than we could ever know individually.

The United States has a long history of gossip in print. Louella Parsons and Hedda Hopper published nationally syndicated newspaper columns that gossiped about Hollywood stars in the 1930s, 1940s, and 1950s. Advice columns like those written by Ann Landers, Carolyn Hax, and Abigail VanBuren involve gossip about more ordinary people. We read them because, even when the advice doesn't apply to us, we enjoy the snapshots they give us into others' lives and dilemmas.

Reading Minds. Henry M. Wellman with Karen Lind, Oxford University Press (2020) © Oxford University Press.
DOI: 10.1093/oso/9780190878672.001.0001

People magazine, which is almost exclusively gossip, grew from these antecedents. *People* is one of the most popular magazines in America. In 2017 it was ranked ninth in circulation. *AARP* was number one, and *Sports Illustrated* was number twelve.

In addition to short pieces like "3 Truths and 1 Lie," *People* devotes longer pieces, replete with quotes, to individuals. A portion of a recent *People* interview with Eva Longoria included the following:

> I was lucky to learn the word "volunteer" at an early age. It was integrated into our family. With the Eva Longoria Foundation I knew I wanted to focus on education. I had researched to see who had the greatest educational disparities in the United States, and it happened to be Latinas. I thought "I'm Latina, and this community needs help."[3]

People was not reporting on itself, it was gossiping about Eva, along with Donald and Melania or the Kardashians. It provides us with glimpses into (or perhaps just speculation about) their minds, thoughts, hopes, disappointments, and dreams.

Although *People* readers are primarily women, it is not just women who listen to and pass along gossip. I'm a subscriber to *Sports Illustrated*, a gossip magazine for sports aficionados and (largely) for men.

In *Sports Illustrated* reporting, rarely is the story solely about the game, the season, or the record achieved. It also is not about the box score or keeping track of who's on the disabled list. Instead, the focus is on how athletes, managers, coaches, and teams deal with those victories, defeats, and injuries. The events provide a springboard to jump into lives, minds, and careers.

Nothing made this more clear than the articles about Super Bowl 50. Would the Denver Broncos win on what was probably Peyton Manning's last shot? When they won, did it validate his career? Was it a fitting final chapter to a dramatic season or to a hall-of-fame career?

The stories traced a saga of Manning remaking himself at age thirty-nine into a quarterback for a very different offensive system. The stories included specifics about his terrible start to the season (seventeen interceptions and only nine touchdowns in nine games); his benching (the first in his professional career); his injury (the last of a long and increasingly frequent list); his revival; and the team's final winning streak, which culminated in a Super Bowl victory.

Then, what about the validation for Broncos general manager John Elway in hiring Manning? And don't forget the backstory of the special relationship forged between Manning and Elway. This is gossip in its widest, and sometimes best, form.

Gossip is only possible because of our theories of mind. Gossip is not just social—we talk with others. It is social cognitive: Through it we learn about people's intentions, quirks, likes, beliefs, deeds, and misdeeds. Gossip—directly in conversation or indirectly via media—reflects our propensity to think about people's actions, lives, and minds. And it illuminates how our theory of mind operates. Gossip is driven by our think–want understandings.

Reading Minds 102

From our earliest years, we try to discover why people are who they are and do what they do. We do this by considering their thoughts, desires, intentions, and feelings. We organize this information into a theory of mind—a framework that helps us make sense of all the pieces.

Our everyday understanding of people is organized around three large categories: their thoughts, their wants, and their actions. We believe that people's thoughts and wants drive their actions. You can see this in the Eva Longoria quotation: "I *wanted* to focus on education. . . . I *thought*, 'I'm Latina and this community needs help.'" Based on her thoughts and wants, she *acted* to establish the Eva Longoria Foundation to "help Latina women improve their lives through education."

Similarly, John Elway *thought* Manning, even nearing forty, had one more Super Bowl victory in him. Elway *wanted* that victory for Denver, the Broncos, and Manning himself. His *action*? He brought Peyton Manning to the Denver Broncos.

Not Just for Experts: Everyday Psychology

Our basic, everyday theory of how people behave is developed from our social interactions and from things like gossip. We don't learn it through formal education, so it doesn't involve egos and ids, therapy and mental illness, brains and hormones. It is ordinary and commonsensical, so it's also called everyday psychology, or intuitive psychology.

In our everyday think–want psychology, thoughts and wants are basic categories that include subtypes and subtleties.

Thoughts Can Include	Wants Can Include
Ideas	Preferences
Knowledge	Hopes
Convictions	Motives
Guesses	Inclinations
Beliefs	Desires
Wonderings	Obligations

From your own experience, you know that thoughts, wants, and actions, even in their expanded versions, don't cover all that goes on. Leading to our thoughts and wants are emotions, urges, and perceptions, and following our actions are reactions. From these many parts we create our theory of mind—our own personal explanation about how the social world functions (Figure 2.1).

Figure 2.2 shows us how this might look for Romeo. Because Romeo *loves* Juliet, he *wants* to be with her. Because he's *seen* his clan's conflict with the Capulets, he *knows* his family will violently object. So he marries Juliet in secret. When he can be with her, he is *ecstatic*. When they are forced to be apart, he is *miserable*.

Theory of Mind

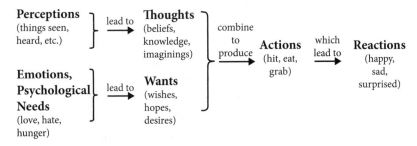

Figure 2.1 The concepts and connections we use to understand human actions and motivations.

Romeo

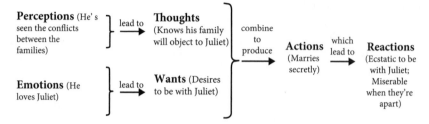

Figure 2.2 The general chart of actions and states shown in Figure 2.1, applied to Romeo.

This framework also allows us to explain and predict behavior. You can move from right to left to explain events or from left to right to predict them.

Explanation: Why does Romeo want to be with Juliet? He *loves* her. Why does he marry her in secret? He's *seen* his clan's conflict with the Capulets and *knows* his family will object violently.

Prediction: What do we expect that Romeo will feel when he and Juliet are wed? He'll be happy, even *ecstatic*. What do we predict Romeo will feel when forced to be apart from Juliet? He'll be *miserable*.

Emotions and physiological states fuel our desires. Perceptions and experiences ground our thoughts. Actions result in outcomes that provoke additional reactions. That's how we think people work, and that's the basis of the immensely powerful framework that helps us make sense of our social world. We use this repeatedly and often unconsciously as we make our way through our social lives. Because we understand this process, we understand *Romeo and Juliet*, gossip, intentions, actions, emotions, thoughts, and desires. It allows us to read minds.

We form many accurate predictions and explanations using our theory of mind. But sometimes we get things wrong, like Romeo did when he thought Juliet was dead. Of course, it's nice to think our explanations are always correct and our predictions entirely accurate. It gives us a sense of security and understanding, reasons we formed a theory of mind in the first place.

But scientists have discovered areas where our explanations and predictions are particularly weak. One notable example, unexpectedly, is an area where we'd like to be accurate and where we feel sure we are. Research shows we are all, across the board and without exception, terrible at detecting liars. Sometimes theory of mind shows us its power by helping us generate cogent predictions and explanations; sometimes it shows us its power by leading us astray.

Lies, Damned Lies, and Deceptions

On February 5, 2003, Colin Powell stood before a plenary session of the United Nations Security Council to argue the U.S. case for military action against Saddam Hussein and Iraq.[4] "There can be no doubt that Saddam Hussein has biological weapons and the capability to produce many, many more," Powell stated.

Further, he said there was "no doubt" in his mind that Saddam was working to acquire nuclear weapons. Saddam was soliciting large quantities of "yellowcake," a type of uranium oxide used to produce nuclear weapons, from Niger. Iraq already had, and was busy acquiring still more, "weapons of mass destruction" (WMDs), Powell said.

Powell's address was particularly forceful because of his background, track record, and status. At 6'2", Powell stood ramrod straight and exuded the authority of the four-star general he was. He had been the youngest chairman of the Joint Chiefs of Staff under President George H. W. Bush and had led Operation Desert Storm, the first U.S. invasion of Iraq. When he stood before the United Nations as George W. Bush's secretary of state, he was a known moderating influence in Bush's cabinet. His military perspective and his expertise as an avowed military "realist" further polished his image. He could not have been more credible.

However, much of what Powell told the United Nations, and thereby the American people, was untrue. Among other errors are the following: There were no stockpiles of WMDs, and Iraq had made no attempt to acquire yellowcake.

Powell was at a vortex of people and events that shaped a "coalition of the willing" to undertake the Second Gulf War. Key players included President Bush; Vice President Cheney; Bush's secretary of defense, Donald Rumsfeld; and others. In retrospect, it is clear that deceptions, lies, and misinformation abounded. To this day, people debate the main players' knowledge, ignorance, roles, and motives in instigating an armed conflict that plagues the Mideast still. Powell's long-time aide-de-camp, Colonel Lawrence

Wilkerson, later said he had unwittingly participated in a hoax on the American people.

When the many instances of misinformation that started the war came to light, a Senate panel investigated. Among other findings, their report detailed intense behind-the-scenes debate in the State Department about Powell's UN speech.

State Department analysts had discovered numerous errors before Powell's speech was delivered, including the false yellowcake claim. Only some of these were corrected. Powell himself later admitted he had presented an inaccurate case to the United Nations. He said the information he had reported was, in some cases, "deliberately misleading."

Perhaps the misrepresentations that remained were the fault of Powell's staff, or perhaps Powell included them knowingly. Well before the speech, in August 1989, *Parade Magazine* had printed Collin Powell's "13 Rules of Leadership." Rule Number 6 was: "Don't let adverse facts stand in the way of a good decision."

My own belief is that Colin Powell was more duped than duper. But whatever the truth, the underlying point is this: Journalists, historians, politicians, and millions of others in the United States and abroad spent untold hours trying to assess the intentions, knowledge, ignorance, desires, doubts, hopes, aspirations, and feelings of the key players. Our thinking about Powell, Bush, Cheney, and others demonstrates a constant, insistent, unavoidable part of our lives. We are compelled to understand people in terms of their inner mental states. We want to read their minds.

"Constant, insistent, unavoidable" is not hyperbole. It may not even capture the importance we place on this kind of thinking. Puzzling over things like Colin Powell's intentions, foreknowledge, beliefs, and decisions represents a vast portion of our everyday moments.

In Powell's case, regardless of whatever else was going on, it is clear he was lied to, probably many times. The reason we suspect him of misinforming us is that we can't believe he didn't spot those lies. He'd had years of experience in reading and evaluating others and in assessing military intelligence and intelligence providers. He had military and political savvy. Surely he, of all people, could spot lies. Yet to the extent he was duped, he did not. To the extent he duped us, we did not.

Why not?

How to Detect Liars

Adults often make judgments about who is lying, and research shows we're confident about those judgments. We understand what lies are—intentions to deceive—and we have a lifetime of experience trying to avoid being taken in. Yet strangely this doesn't lead to expertise. We become experienced but not expert.

Most people have a theory of mind about spotting liars that goes something like this: Lying makes the liar's mind churn. (Maybe I'll get caught. I have to be vigilant to make sure I stick to my made-up story.) This makes the liar nervous and tense. And this nervous tension makes people hesitate, sweat, fidget, and avoid eye contact. Research shows that virtually all of us believe this—but we're wrong.

In a frequently used research procedure, people are videotaped talking about an event they witnessed. Some describe it truthfully; some lie. The tapes are then shown to other adults who try to assess if the person on tape was lying or telling the truth.

Assessors in these studies, and in other related ones, are generally quite confident in determining who lied. They say the liars shifted their gaze and had fidgety, nervous actions.

Around the globe, assessors point to these same behaviors as indicating liars. Charles Bond, a social psychologist at Texas Christian University who has published widely in psychology and statistics, writes that in fifty-one of fifty-eight countries, people most often link deception with a shifting gaze. People also cite increased body movements, fidgeting, and postural changes, as well as a higher pitched voice and speech errors, as indicating lies. So we're clear and consistent in pinpointing what lying looks like. It's as clear as the nose on Pinocchio's face.

Yet despite our certainty, hundreds of studies show that we're hopeless at spotting lies or liars. Some of these studies have used videotape; some used face-to-face presentations; some tested run-of-the-mill college students; some tested "experts" like police officers or interrogation specialists. In all of the studies, subjects failed repeatedly and abysmally to pinpoint who lied and who told the truth.

Bella DePaulo, an Italian scientist who has studied deception for more than twenty years, joined forces with Charles Bond to aggregate all these data into one megastudy, termed a *meta-analysis*.[5] Summing the many, many studies, adults averaged 54 percent correct judgments about who was lying. That is, their judgments were only microscopically better than the 50 percent judgments that would be achieved by random guessing. And experts, like police officers, who routinely assess lying in their jobs, performed no better than untrained twenty-year-olds.

These results may seem questionable given our massive agreement about how liars behave. And they could be misleading—the studies are far removed from real life. Maybe the studies seemed so unimportant that the assessors didn't really try.

Paul Ekman and his colleagues ran a study that addressed this.[6] Ekman is professor emeritus at the University of California Medical School in San Francisco. Over the course of his forty-year career he has become well known in scientific circles and well known to police officers, the Federal Bureau of Investigation, and the Secret Service for assistance in serious "lie catching," as he calls it.

Early in his career, he conducted a study with nursing students. He set up a situation where it was difficult for them to conceal real feelings and beliefs, but important that they do so. Ekman's instructions to the students tell the story:

> If you are working in an emergency room and a mother rushes in with a badly mangled child, you can't show your distress even if you know the child is in terrible pain and has little chance to survive. You have to hold your own feelings in and calm the mother down until the doctor comes. This experiment offers you a chance to test out and practice your ability.
>
> First, you will see a pleasant film showing colorful ocean scenes, and while you watch it you are to describe your feelings frankly to an interviewer who cannot see which film you are watching. Then you will see some of the very worst scenes you may ever encounter in your years of nursing experience. While you watch those scenes you will have to conceal your real feelings so that the interviewer will think you are seeing another pleasant film. You can say it is showing pretty flowers in Golden State Park. Try as hard as you can.

The gruesome film he showed them was of a burn patient in severe pain spliced with a film of a difficult, bloody, surgical amputation to look like the burn patient also needed an amputation. Ekman said they were "the very worst films we could find."

Because the nursing students were early in their training, they were new to gruesome events and also to giving sometimes-necessary deceptions. This would seem to make the lie detectors' task easier. On the other hand, the students were motivated to succeed in their training, and this was a relevant training experience. And although the students were acting, they were acting in a task where they saw real-life consequences of their actions. In short, this was a fair and convincing test.

A few of the students were terrible liars and so were easily detected. But most of the students misled their judges. These judges were told nothing about the setup and were asked just to make a simple decision: whether the students were describing the film honestly or dishonestly. Very few of the observers were better than chance at figuring that out.

Another set of judges was made more suspicious. They were told the two scenarios the students might see on film, but not which film the students were seeing. These "suspicious" viewers performed about as poorly as the uninformed judges.

If we assume Colin Powell was duped by others in the lead-up to his UN address, he was in good company. In the ordinary course of events, we're just not good at detecting lies, even when we have reason to be suspicious.

But why not? We have vast experience both in reading lies and, probably, in telling them. We spend large parts of our social interaction reading minds—and doing it accurately. Why can't we get this right?

Because people's theory of mind about lying—in this case their conviction about how lying affects behavior—is wrong. Lying doesn't lead to shifting eye movement or to fidgeting, no matter how many of us believe it does. Because this is a surprisingly widespread and powerful false belief, it reinforces a key feature of theory of mind: It is theory not fact. We assemble our theories from facts, observations, hypotheses, and ideas to give us orderly understandings, and sometimes the picture we assemble is wrong.

Knowing who the liars and truth-tellers were, scientists reanalyzed videotapes to determine what liars really do. The bottom line is this: Gaze aversion and nervous fidgeting—the two behaviors that thousands worldwide pointed to as indicating liars—didn't distinguish the liars versus the truth tellers.

Bella DePaulo and her colleagues checked this finding using another meta-analysis. Across 100 studies involving thousands of adults, gaze aversion did not predict lying, and nervous behaviors—fidgeting, blushing, stuttering—didn't either.

In spite of these findings, stereotypes of lying behaviors persist, even in those with training and experience. Law enforcement officers often say that lying suspects avoid looking them in the eye, shift their gaze, tap fingers, hesitate to answer, and get more and more nervous as an interview goes on. Freud said a liar "chatters with his finger-tips; betrayal oozes out of him at every pore."

But research shows that people who are telling the truth also do these things. They avoid eye contact, especially with police officers (they don't want to appear confrontational); they shift their gaze (for example, looking up into space as they try to recall where they were and what they were doing); hesitate (wanting to be correct and precise); and they get nervous (worrying that the officer could be—is!—suspecting them even though they had nothing to do with the events in question).

Tom Brokaw, for many years anchor of NBC's *Nightly News* and a tough interviewer for the *Today Show,* said he vigilantly looked for people hiding unwanted truths. "Most of the clues I get from people are verbal not physical. I don't look at a person's face for signs that he is lying. What I'm after are convoluted answers or sophisticated evasions."

Yet even this highly trained analyst and interviewer is wrong. Research shows that when lying, some people use circumlocution and give more information than requested, but many are just the opposite: direct and nonevasive. Moreover, many truthful people happen to be convoluted and long-winded; it's just the way they talk.

In sum, our cues for lying point equally to the guilty and the innocent alike, although that is not what we believe. Despite years of being concerned about lying, most adults' theories about lying are wrong (Sidebar 2.1).

The obvious point here is that our theories of mind can fail us. We can hold, and act on, beliefs that are incorrect. The less obvious point is that we are so driven to understand the mental workings of others that we make theories about them, even wrong ones, rather than interact without any theory at all.

Sidebar 2.1 Looking for Lies in All the Wrong Places

Can nobody detect liars?
The century-old polygraph, the "lie detector," definitely cannot. For a polygraph test, subjects are asked a series of questions while hooked to electrodes that record responses like respiration, heart rate, and skin resistance. Polygraphs measure changes in arousal, but liars can remain

mostly unaroused, while innocents can be worried and aroused by target questions that can expose them to gruesome details or make them fear they are under suspicion.

Paul Ekman, who conducted the research with the student nurses, thinks he can detect lies and can train others to do so. The key, he claims, is careful expert analysis of emotions expressed in body language, tone of voice, and, critically, "microexpressions" that pass fleetingly across the facial muscles. Ekman is justly famous for his analyses of human facial expressions. Through painstaking investigation, he and his colleagues created FACS, the Facial Action Coding System, to describe all the observable movements that animate our emotional expressions. Ekman's research on microexpression was spotlighted in Malcom Gladwell's book, *Blink,* and he consulted on the TV series *Lie to Me.* Ekman developed METT (Micro-Expressions Training Tool) to help individuals learn to use FACS to analyze fleeting emotions. Ekman claims that METT can increase accuracy in detecting truthfulness in law enforcement.

Ekman's work on emotion is highly regarded, but his claims about lie detecting are much more controversial. Part of Ekman's claims for the METT came from research on "truth wizards," individuals who were consistently above chance in spotting lies. The Wizards Project began with 20,000 persons and found only 50 who could consistently spot deception without training. This fraction is so small it could represent random chance. Weigh against this the voluminous data that show that even trained experts can't spot lies, as we saw in the meta-analyses of Bella DePaulo and her colleagues.

So the short answer to the question, can we detect liars? Not consistently, not reliably, not yet.

Our Social Brain

When we gossip, when we struggle with who is lying and who is not, when we appreciate Shakespeare's tragedy, and even when we understand Glenda's simple mistaken belief, we are taking part in one of the wonders of our mental world. We are employing our species' remarkable, powerful ability to read minds. And we do it without telepathy, or the Tarot, or brain scanners. We use our ever-ready theory of mind.

Nicholas Humphrey, a British psychologist known for his work on the evolution of human intelligence, claimed humans should not be characterized as *Homo sapiens* but as *Homo psychologicus*:

> The ability to do psychology is by no means an ordinary ability in the animal kingdom. Yet far from being something which baffles human understanding, the open discussion of one's inner experience is literally child's play to a human being, children begin to learn it before they are more than two or three years old. And the fact that this common-sense is acquired so easily suggests that this is natural to human beings.[7]

He argued that the basis of our overall human intelligence was our distant ancestors' increasing ability to think about the social world. This is now called the "social brain" hypothesis.

Humphrey posited that human intelligence arose because protohumans lived in an increasingly complex social world. Social life placed a premium on understanding allies as well as competitors because they could aid or thwart access to food, mating, and social status. Better understanding of allies and enemies then promoted increased social life and social reasoning.

Robin Dunbar also argued for the social brain hypothesis. He hypothesized that gossip—our human need to talk to each other about each other—is a cause as well as a consequence of the evolution of our intelligence and language. Theory of mind, these scientists said, is powerful not only because we use it every day for thinking and talking about people but also because it has shaped the ways we have come to think.

I argue that additionally, and better yet, theory of mind is not just a product of evolutionary development, it is a product of childhood development. Our theory of mind is formulated from experiences and learning that accumulate over the course of our lives and interactions, but it takes root and its power emerges in childhood. *Reading Minds* focuses on childhood not because kids are cute and amusing, but because understanding how theory of mind develops is the only way to really understand the theory and the best way to understand ourselves and our social world.

The rest of this book tells that story: We *are*, because we *become*, *Homo psychologicus*. And it all begins with children.

3

Friends, Secrets, and Lies

In 1954 the U.S. Supreme Court mandated that public schools could no longer be segregated. Louisiana as a state, and New Orleans as a city, refused to comply with the ruling until 1960, when federal marshals enforced desegregation.

The process began in two New Orleans first grades. Three black children were sent to the previously all-white McDonogh School, and a single six-year-old girl, Ruby Bridges, was sent to the previously all-white William Frantz School. The integration was labeled in the news as the "New Orleans School Desegregation Crisis."[1]

Ruby herself was not so much in the news; to protect her, her name was not released until many years later. But reporters flocked to write about the "Cheerleaders"—a group of white middle-aged women, along with their children, who were boycotting the William Frantz School in protest. The Cheerleaders were fierce.

In his book, *Travels with Charley*, John Steinbeck described their language as "bestial, and filthy and degenerate." As Ruby walked into school flanked by four large U.S. marshals, one woman threatened to poison her, and another held up a child-size coffin holding a black doll. Steinbeck was so sickened by the demonstrations against this "small dark mite" that he watched for half an hour "and got out of town."

But the Cheerleaders were effective. In 1959, William Frantz had an enrollment of 550 children; by November of the year Ruby attended, enrollment had dropped to 3.

Ruby was in a classroom by herself with a single teacher, Barbara Henry, the only teacher in the building willing to teach in a desegregated classroom. Ruby believed she was alone in the entire school and did not learn until the following spring that "three or four" first graders were being taught in a separate classroom. Ruby ate lunch in her room and had no recess, so she had no contact with anyone at the school except her teacher.

Near the end of her first-grade year, when a few more white children returned to school, Ruby got the chance to visit with them on the playground

Reading Minds. Henry M. Wellman with Karen Lind, Oxford University Press (2020) © Oxford University Press.
DOI: 10.1093/oso/9780190878672.001.0001

"once or twice." At the time Ruby knew little about peer racism. She'd grown up in a segregated black neighborhood and went to a segregated kinder-garten. "The light dawned one day when a little white boy refused to play with me. 'I can't play with you,' the boy said. 'My mama said not to 'cause you're a nigger.'"

Ruby's first-grade year was nothing any child should experience. She walked to school each morning amid invective, shouting, and threats. She was isolated in her classroom and was an outcast on the playground. Crucially, from a developmental standpoint, Ruby was friendless.

Research findings on this are very clear: Being friendless can have disas-trous consequences for a child's social and academic life that can continue into adulthood.

> Being friendless has numerous negative consequences, including low self-worth, social anxiety, depression, loneliness and suicidal ideation.[2]

Yet somehow Ruby succeeded. She married, had children, had a successful career, and in 1999 established the Ruby Bridges Foundation to promote "the values of tolerance, respect, and appreciation of all differences."

How did she manage this when so many factors were stacked against her?

Being buffered from peer problems is closely related to a child's theory-of-mind abilities. We know this because of research where false-belief tests, like the one when a child predicts where Glenda will look for candy, are used to evaluate a child's theory-of-mind abilities. Preschool children with the best false-belief understanding are more popular and better accepted in Israel, Australia, the United Kingdom, the United States, Canada, and many other locales where this has been studied.[3]

As well as acquiring friends and avoiding friendlessness, theory-of-mind advances impact a child's ability to keep secrets, to inform (and deceive) others, and to persuade and argue, all skills vital to a person's social well-being. False-belief studies provide a key window for seeing how theory of mind can affect children's, and then adults', lives.

Children Master False Beliefs

Preschoolers in developed countries show how understanding false beliefs impacts their own behavior and thinking. This understanding has also been shown to impact their interpretation of the behavior and thinking of others. And, to repeat, this has immense and long-lasting consequences for their well-being.

But is this understanding something children everywhere learn? If not, it would be less consequential than I've suggested because children everywhere grow up to be competent social interactors.

Back to Africa

The Baka are hunter–gatherers of the central African rainforest. They are a small people, with the larger adult males standing about five feet tall. They were once called Pygmies, a term first used by ancient Egyptians that is now considered disrespectful and stigmatizing.

The Baka are seminomadic and set up temporary forest camps where the men trap, fish, and hunt, often using poison-tipped arrows. The women cultivate squashes, cassavas, and bananas, and they gather other food like wild mango and honey.

In 1990, two Oxford researchers, Jeremy Avis and Paul Harris, tested Baka children on their false-belief understandings.[4] They worked in the children's home camps, using a skit enacted by two Baka experimenters, Mopfana, an adolescent male, and Mobissa, an older man. Children ranging in age from very young three-year-olds to six-year-olds were tested.

For the task, each child came to a camp hut with his or her mother. Mopfana and Mobissa sat by a fire where Mopfana roasted wild mango kernels, a Baka delicacy. Beside the fire stood a lidded bowl and a lidded pot, and inside the hut were other common items like a basket and a pile of clothes.

The children sat on Mobissa's knee and watched while Mopfana took the kernels off the fire and placed them in the bowl. Then Mopfana dramatically said, "Look at these tasty kernels I've cooked here; they're so sweet, so sugary, so delicious! Yum."

"But before I eat them I need to go over to the *mbanjo* [the male meeting hut] for a quick smoke. I'll be back to eat them soon." Then Mopfana covered the bowl and the pot with their lids and left the child with their mother and Mobissa.

Because he was older, Mobissa had higher status than Mopfana, which helped legitimate the next part of the skit. Mobissa said, "Mopfana has gone and can't see what we're doing. C'mon, let's play a game. Take the kernels from the bowl and hide them. Where do you think we should hide them?"

Many of the children spontaneously hid the kernels in the pot or in the pile of clothes. If a child didn't hide the kernels or didn't hide them effectively, Mobissa said, "Put them in the pot."

Then he said, "There, the kernels are in the pot" (or wherever) and asked the child three questions:

1. "When Mopfana comes back, where will he look for the kernels, in the bowl or in the pot?" This is a classic false-belief question. A child should say, like adults do, that Mopfana will look in the bowl because that's where he left them. Mopfana would have a false belief and act on it.

Then the children were asked a second question:

2. "When Mopfana goes to the bowl, before he lifts the lid off the bowl, will his heart feel good or bad?" If children understand Mopfana's belief, they should say he'll feel good because he (falsely) thinks he is about to get delicious kernels.

Finally, the children were asked:

3. "After he lifts the lid, will Mopfana's heart feel good or bad?" This is a control question to ensure the child remembers the events and the fact that the bowl is empty. If they do, when Mopfana lifts the lid to find an empty bowl, he will feel sad or angry, his "heart will feel bad." Almost all of the children at all ages answered this third question correctly.

But on the first two questions, the children's accuracy varied hugely by age. The older children (ages four-and-a-half to six) answered questions 1 and 2 correctly almost 90 percent of the time—vastly above chance. The younger children (ages three to four-and-a-half) were no better than chance.

These findings are almost identical to the findings from the candy box task from Chapter 1. In spite of huge cultural and geographic differences, at about age four-and-a-half, children make an enormous leap of understanding. Before that age most cannot understand that a person could hold a belief that is false; after that age, most can (see Sidebar 3.1).[5]

Sidebar 3.1 More About False Beliefs

Figure 3.1 shows a meta-analysis that incorporates more than 250 studies of children's understanding of false beliefs.[5] If children chose randomly between two choices (Mopfana could look in either the bowl or the pot), they would be correct 50 percent of the time, which on this graph would be a score of 0.

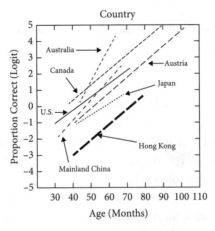

Figure 3.1 Children proceed more quickly or more slowly, but in all locales, young children go from below- to above-chance performance.

But the graph shows something very different. With increasing age, children shift from making consistent false-belief errors (below 0) to responding consistently above chance (above 0). That was true of the Baka, and it's true of the more than 8,000 children from different countries whose responses are aggregated in this figure. Understanding false beliefs is a major, widespread milestone as preschoolers develop a theory of mind.

Some of the tasks used in the graph were about changed locations (like the mango kernels) and some about deceptive contents (a plain box that holds candy and a candy box that does not). Some required a verbal response; some, like the Baka's task, could be answered with a point. Some asked children to judge behavior (Where will Mopfana look?); some asked about thoughts (What does Mopfana think?) or emotions (Will Mopfana's heart feel good or bad?). Some asked children to judge live humans (like Mopfana), some used videotape, some used puppets or story characters. The differences in the task made virtually no difference in the outcomes: All the children answered in the same ways.

But there *are* differences in the age when children learn this skill. Some children are faster or slower to achieve false-belief understanding, and that difference impacts their social lives and interactions.

Nonetheless, as Figure 3.1 also shows, children's think--want understanding, as shown by their understanding of false beliefs, changes substantially in the preschool years. Yet, the pint-size tot who has figured this out is probably still learning to kick a ball and ride a bike.

To have learned so much so young suggests these understandings are vital to a child's competence.

Lies and Deception

Tom Sawyer is one of the most enduring characters in American fiction. He is brash, persuasive, untruthful, and imaginative, and he demonstrates one of the most robust theories of mind in literature.

The Adventures of Tom Sawyer, by Mark Twain, opens with Tom telling a whopper. One hot afternoon he skipped school to go swimming. Through careful misrepresentation, he has almost convinced his Aunt Polly, who raises him, that he hasn't done it. Then his half-brother, Sid, pipes up, saying Tom's shirt is on differently than it had been that morning. Tom races out of the house before he can be punished.

No parent likes to think they've raised a liar, and Aunt Polly scolds herself for not being harder on Tom. "Spare the rod and spile the child, as the Good Book says."

But wrong as it may seem, lying is an important step forward in a child's growth and is an important social skill. Imagine a world where people always blurted out the unvarnished truth: "That's the ugliest paint job I ever saw." "Your hair looks dreadful that way." Or in childhood, isn't everyone happier when Grandma gives her granddaughter a sweater and the child says, "Thank you, Grandma. It's just what I wanted," instead of the truth, "But I wanted a Barbie."

Life would be harder without the social niceties that arise from not always blabbing out the truth, that is, without lying. But children aren't born lying, and they're certainly not born telling white lies. My younger brother once blurted out to a first-time babysitter, "Boy you have a long, skinny neck." She never returned.

How and when do children learn this somewhat dubious skill? How do they become more socialized beings in this way?

When asked, most parents say their children began to lie at about four years. Their lies involve false denials ("I didn't do it"); false blame ("He did it"); false claims ("Dad said it's OK"); false boasts ("I can do that, too"); and false ignorance ("I don't know who broke it").

Scientists have spent great effort trying to determine why lying begins at this age. Is it because language gets better, which it does? Or that children get smarter, which they do? In fact, lying is primarily a function of a child's improved theory of mind. Lying and deception emerge and increase hand in hand with a child's understanding of false belief.

To reach this conclusion, scientists had to sort through considerable chaff. For example, parents of two- and three-year-olds also report times when their child falsely denies having done something or falsely inflates some boast to outsize proportions. But if theory of mind is correct, children shouldn't be able to lie in those ways before about age four-and-a-half. At age two or three, they couldn't read another's thoughts well enough to manipulate them with deception.

To find out what is really going on, researchers have used a "temptation" task. Billy (or Annie) watches as an adult places a gift the child can't see in a container "for later." Then the adult leaves the room, telling the child not to peek. The children are watched through a one-way mirror or are videotaped. In one classic study, almost 90 percent of the two- and three-year-old children peeked to see the gift.

When the adult returns, the adult asks the child, "Did you peek?" About half the preschoolers say "no," which seems like a lie. This is a large percentage of apparent liars, although this percentage grows far higher for older children. By age five, about 80 percent of the children lie.

Further studies have explained this difference and show why those young children who didn't understand others' beliefs look like liars. The very youngest children aren't trying to deceive the experimenter; they are trying to avoid punishment.

If Mom points to a broken vase and says, "Did you do that?" (or if an experimenter asks, "Did you peek?"), a child might say "no" to get out of trouble (such as failure to get the gift). Even a very young child can recognize that the person who causes the problem can get in hot water. Deny causing the problem and you avoid unwanted repercussions. This requires understanding cause and effect, but not, necessarily, understanding how others think. Running away or simply grabbing the prize could accomplish the same things: avoiding the bad or getting the good. Lying, however, is more: It's *intending* to plant mistaken *belief* to avoid getting the bad or to facilitate getting the good.

To better understand what is going on, researchers at the University of Toronto, led by Kang Lee, studied what happens when the child foresees no serious consequences.[6] Lee and his colleagues placed an object—a purple toy Barney—behind children so they couldn't see it. The children were told not to peek at it when the adult left the room, but no gifts or possible disappointments were mentioned. After videoing whether children actually peeked, the adult interviewed the children. Once punishment was ruled out, the child's understanding of others' beliefs predicted lying, with correlations* ranging from .40 to .70, as measured using standard false-belief tests.

To put this in perspective, think about the correlation between height and shoe size in adults. Sensibly enough, taller people on average have bigger feet. But there also is slippage: There are big people with small feet, diminutive people with large ones. The correlation between height and shoe size is usually about .60 or so. Statistically, it's strong. Equally, the correlation between false-belief understanding and lying is statistically strong (Sidebar 3.2).

Sidebar 3.2 From Correlation to Causation

Because something is substantially correlated with something else does not prove that one causes the other. For example, working crossword puzzles correlates with better memory and cognitive functioning in late life. Does this prove that doing crossword puzzles protects against cognitive decline? No, older adults who do crosswords are on average better educated and better off financially than those who do not, and it is education and financial resources that impact cognitive health in older adults.

Researchers use several steps to try to determine when a factor causes (not just correlates with) a result. Crucially, they consider which other

---

* Correlations between two factors—lying and false-belief understanding—can vary from 0 to 1.0 (or technically from −1.0 through 0 to 1.0), where 1.0 means a perfect prediction. In this case, each stepwise increment in understanding false belief (as children get older and older) is matched by a comparable increment in, say, lying. Roughly, correlations from 0 to .10 are essentially absent; false belief didn't predict lying in any meaningful way. Correlations from .10 to .30 are weak. Correlations from .30 to the .50s are large, and correlations above .50 are strong and become stronger the higher they get. So a correlation of .40 (which occurs in several of Lee's studies of false belief understanding predicting lying) is large, and one of .70 (in other studies) is strong indeed.

factors should be ruled out. In the case of testing a link between false-belief understanding and lying in childhood, they often consider general intelligence, language competence, and "executive functioning," which refers to the processes we use to deliberately control our actions and words. All of these increase in the preschool years along with the child's developing theory of mind and their lying.

But false-belief reasoning remains as a powerful predictor of children's lying, even when all the other abilities—IQ, language competence, and executive functioning—are eliminated.

Theory of mind gives us the power of controlling others' knowledge. And lying is just the tip of the iceberg.

Hiding and Secrets

Tom Sawyer and his friend Huck Finn visit a graveyard at midnight, carrying a dead cat. They plan to use a sure-fire cure to remove warts: They will throw the cat at the headstone of an evil person and chant

> Devil follow corpse,
> Cat follow devil,
> Warts follow cat,
> I'm done with ye.

But before they can begin, they witness a fight between three grave robbers. By the end of it, Injun Joe has killed a man. But he leaves the murder weapon, a knife, in the hand of Muff Potter, who has been knocked unconscious during the fight.

When the murder is discovered, Injun Joe testifies that Potter did the killing. Tom and Huck know this is untrue but are terrified of what Injun Joe might do to them if they tell, so they keep his secret. Although they remain silent, Twain explained, "The dreadful secret of the murder was a chronic misery."

Secrets are as vital to social interaction as they are to fiction, and they can be positive. A secret can create closeness, as when a teenaged girl tells only her best friend she's in love with the school bad boy.

The fundamental element in secrets is that one person must be kept ignorant of something another person knows. Most of us can recount a time when a child couldn't manage it. On my birthday, my three-year-old grandson and his mother wrapped a present for me. As soon as I walked in their door, he said, "It's a book."

Joan Peskin and Vittoria Ardino studied children's secret keeping.[7] Preschool children helped hide a birthday cake from an adult teacher in their school kitchen. They were told repeatedly, "It's a secret. Don't tell." A child was then left alone with the teacher in the kitchen.

Only 30 percent of the three-year-olds kept the secret, while 70 percent of the four-year-olds and 90 percent of the five-year-olds did so. There was a strong correlation between a child's performance on a battery of false-belief tests and keeping a secret—a correlation of .62. That is, children who better understood false beliefs were better at keeping knowledge from a third person. Children's theories of mind are progressively maturing over the preschool years, and this has important and predictable consequences for their social actions—like secret keeping—and their lives.

Persuasion

As punishment for skipping school, Tom Sawyer is ordered to whitewash the front fence. He sulks and procrastinates, but then figures out how to manage his friends' beliefs by persuading them that whitewashing is a desirable thing. "Does a boy get a chance to whitewash a fence every day?" and "I reckon there ain't one boy in a thousand, maybe two thousand, that can do it the way it's got to be done," Tom says.

Soon, Tom has his friends painting his fence and paying him for the privilege, while he remains idle all afternoon. We might wish we had his persuasive talent.

Children's earliest attempts at persuasion can be simple pleas ("please, pretty please") or tears. If these strategies are learned by rote, as when the child mimics an older sibling, they would not involve theory of mind. But adult-like persuasion most often requires speaking to listeners' beliefs.

Karen Bartsch and her colleagues at the University of Wyoming have tried to sort out which persuasions are learned by rote and which rely on managing information (childhood spin-doctoring), the way Tom's did.[8] In their studies, children first saw a replica of a puppy who was "very gentle and really quiet." A puppet, Tricia, came along and was told, "Tricia, the puppy wants you to pet him."

Tricia says, "Oh no, because I think puppies bite."

The child was then asked what to say to Tricia to get her to pet the puppy: "Should we tell Tricia that the puppy is gentle or that the puppy is quiet?"

A second puppet, Chris, came in. He didn't want to pet the puppy either, this time because, "I think puppies bark too loud." Again the child was asked whether to tell Chris that the puppy is gentle or that it's quiet.

Would children understand enough about the puppets' concerns to persuade Tricia and Chris using different arguments? If a child could do this, it would indicate a clear use of persuasion based on the listener's beliefs.

In this and in several related studies, three-year-olds performed essentially at chance, four-year-olds performed better than chance, and five-year-olds performed better still.

Bartsch and her collaborators also showed that this sort of interactive persuasion correlated with false-belief understanding. Correlations for that were .50 for three-year-olds and .70 for four- or five-year-olds. In fact, a child's understanding of false beliefs was a prerequisite for convincingly persuading others. Children who were good persuaders were invariably good at false belief.

Ruby Bridges and Friendlessness

So, what does all this have to do with Ruby Bridges? Young children who best understand false beliefs not only are better liars, secret keepers, and persuaders but also are more popular and better accepted by their peers.

In thieir recent meta-analysis, Virginia Slaughter and her University of Queensland colleagues reviewed this research.[9] They included twenty separate studies that involved more than 2,000 children from preschools, kindergartens, and early primary grades in ten different countries. Theory of mind correlated with peer popularity in all countries. When background factors like gender and age were eliminated, better theory-of-mind understanding (mostly better false-belief understanding) still consistently and significantly predicted better peer acceptance. More crucial still, children who were better at reading minds were buffered from friendlessness at school.

Peer unpopularity and peer friendlessness are not the same. Children who are generally unpopular or ignored by their school group can have one school friend who reciprocates their friendship—a mutual friend—and feel content. In reverse, some children can be highly popular in a group but have no mutual friend and feel lonely and dissatisfied. They are friendless.

In a recent study, Marc de Rosnay and his colleagues looked at the transition from preschool to first grade, a crucial time in a child's social life and peer relationships.[10] They found that children with the best theory of mind skills in preschool were buffered from friendlessness: They might not be popular but they made at least one good friend in the transition to school. And that single relationship mitigated the "low self-worth, social anxiety, depression, loneliness and suicidal ideation" that can result from friendlessness.

Bridges has written about her kindergarten year, the year before she entered the desegregated William Frantz School. She went to Johnson Lockett Elementary School along with all the other kids on her block. As Ruby said in her book, *Through My Eyes*, "I loved school that year, and my teacher, Mrs. King, was warm and encouraging. She was black, as all teachers in black schools were back then. Mrs. King reminded me of my grandmother."

Then she began her year of friendlessness. Ruby, as she described in her autobiography, began to have nightmares, and she developed eating difficulties. She ate her lunch by herself in her classroom, "Mrs. Henry took her lunch break with the other teachers." Ruby began throwing her sandwiches away in a storage cabinet and pouring her carton of milk into a big jar of white paste. At home, all she wanted to eat were potato chips and soda.

Once the school year was over, Ruby went for the summer to her grandmother's farm, along with numerous cousins. Her eating difficulties disappeared. "I took those summers for granted then, the way kids do, but I know now they were a gift." Other children, black and white, joined her classrooms in the following years. Ruby went on to a successful life.

How did she succeed? We can only make an educated guess. Perhaps her theory of mind was so well developed by age six, when she started at the William Frantz School, that she could employ social insights to overcome the friendlessness along with the taunts and insults. Perhaps she succeeded because she had friends in her neighborhood or among her cousins. Or perhaps it was because, even at school, Ruby was not friendless; she has described Mrs. Henry as "my teacher and best friend."

4

Imagination and Reality

At age two, Mary had an imaginary companion named Tagar. She led him around on an imaginary string and put imaginary food for him under the radiator where he slept. "Berrie" and "Auntie" joined Tagar when Mary was three-and-a-half. They quickly became members of the family. She set places for them at the table and asked if they'd eaten enough, she took them on family outings, and she insisted her friends talk with them on the phone. Unlike Mary herself, they were never punished because they never did anything wrong.

About 30 percent of preschoolers in the United States have an imaginary companion. This one was documented by Margaret Svendsen in 1934.[1] Marjorie Taylor, a psychologist at the University of Oregon who studies imaginary companions in contemporary children,[2] has heard about many others:

Joshua was an opossum who lived miles south of the child in San Francisco.

Hekka was a three-year-old invisible boy who talked a lot and was sometimes mean.

A forty-year-old remembered his boyhood companions, Digger and Dewgy. Dewgy was a dog who talked, cracked jokes, and liked rough and tumble play. Digger was brave and daring and protected the boy and protected Dewgy. He "designed the roads in the sandbox, and tempted me to stay when my mother called me home."

One parent told Taylor about her son's playmate, Nobby, who she described as a little invisible boy. When Taylor interviewed the child, she asked how often he played with Nobby. The boy scowled and replied, "I don't *play* with him." Nobby was a 160-year-old businessman who visited the boy between business trips to Seattle and Portland. He stopped by when the boy wanted to "talk things over." Even his mother hadn't known.

Reading Minds. Henry M. Wellman with Karen Lind, Oxford University Press (2020) © Oxford University Press.
DOI: 10.1093/oso/9780190878672.001.0001

As a preschooler, I had an invisible companion named Mr. Nobody. He was a naughty boy slightly older than me. He was short-lived, but very handy. I blamed him for everything that went wrong.

Imaginary companions appear in many forms. Hobbes, in Bill Watterson's classic comic strip *Calvin and Hobbes*, is a famous example of an imaginary companion in stuffed animal form. To anyone else, Hobbes was Calvin's beat up and inert stuffed tiger. In Calvin's mind (and Watterson's strip), he was full of reckless abandon, often egging Calvin on to trouble. A. A. Milne's *Winnie the Pooh* holds a world of imaginary companions modeled on stuffed animals. Milne's son, Christopher Robin Milne, had a bear named Edward who inspired Pooh's personality.

Taylor has found that imaginary companions can have physical form, like these stuffed animals, or they can be purely mental creations. Or a child might invent an imaginary identity to become a superhero or a fairy princess or might transform into a unique being like "Mr. Electricity" or "Flashman of the World." Typically, imaginary companions have ideas, emotions, and desires separate from the child's. Digger was full of daring, Mr. Nobody made mischief, and Hekka was mean in act and intent.

It's not unusual for a companion to be mean to or to scare the child who imagines it. In Taylor's book, *Imaginary Companions and the Children Who Create Them,* one mother reported that from ages three to five her son had an imaginary "bad guy," Barnaby, who lived in his bedroom closet. Barnaby was big, had a black mustache, and "liked to scare people." Her son often asked his mother to check in his closet to see if Barnaby was there. She always said no, but the child was not reassured; after all, Barnaby was invisible. Unfortunately, Barnaby was crafty, too. During an airplane trip the mother told her son Barnaby would not be at the new place because he wasn't on the plane. Her son said Barnaby was following on the next flight.

Often an imaginary companion becomes a real presence in the family's, as well as the child's, life—a personage with its own feelings or ideas. Our son, Trey, accumulated four stuffed alligator Bouffies in the final count. Every one had the same in-your-face personality, which our entire family acknowledged and accepted. We usually allowed Trey to bring only one Bouffie with us on trips—even one went a long way. In advance of one trip, I heard Trey telling all of them together which Bouffie could come and telling him not to brag, it would hurt the others' feelings.

These companions may be treated as if they were real, but young children are clear they're imagined. In my laboratory at the University of Michigan, sometimes a child will bring along a stuffed animal companion when they visit for a study. Sometimes I explain to the animal how the study will work, a good way to tell the child twice. I also ask the animal for their explanation of what happened in the task after I've asked the child, which can helpfully elicit further explanations from the child. I've often had children interrupt me to make sure I understand, "He's not for real," or, "We're only pretending. He can't really talk."

Marjorie Taylor reports the same thing has happened in her laboratory in Oregon. When she has been interviewing a child about his or her imaginary companions, the child will stop her to explain, "It's just pretend, you know?"

Taylor described a boy named Dickie who created an imaginary farm full of imaginary animals. At one family reunion, some of Dickie's relatives, who had seen Dickie's imaginary play before, had a long discussion about the farm and its animals. Dickie approached his father and whispered to him, "Tell them it isn't a real farm."

Real or Imagined: Can Children Tell?

These stories suggest that children with imaginary companions can track the line between the imagined and the real, at least in the case of their "special friends." But, can they do this generally? An adult easily builds castles in the air—dreams combined with ideas and memories—and we know these have less substance than a cobweb. We also know they bear little resemblance to a stone-and-mortar castle from the twelfth century.

But, can a child understand this? After all, both a real dog and the idea of a dog are processed through the brain. Maybe there's a tangle of real and unreal that becomes clear only with time and experience. How or when does a child know the difference between a physical thing and a mental one?

Jean Piaget

Jean Piaget began to study this question in the 1920s. Piaget is an iconic figure in child development. Often, he is pictured with his unruly white hair, sitting amid innumerable piles of papers and books in his incredibly messy office, smoking a pipe. Or, he's pictured on his bike wearing a beret, pedaling around Geneva, Switzerland, (and still smoking his pipe).

Piaget is one of a long line of famous Swiss reformers, so renowned the Swiss erected a bronze bust of him in Bastions Park in Geneva, among other reformers like theologian John Calvin. Piaget's call for reform came in psychology and philosophy.[3] He argued that if you want to understand how the human mind works, you must see how it forms over development. I agree.

Piaget's research with children fills more than forty books and includes studies with hundreds of children along with detailed diaries on his own three children. In one, he describes his daughter's imaginary friend, Aseau, who shape-changed into a bird, a dog, or even a monster.

Piaget persuasively claimed that mental entities, such as ideas, thoughts, imaginings, and memories, are impossibly confusing for young children because they are insubstantial and nonobvious. Preschoolers, he said, are "realists" who see mental entities as tangible, physical objects. He said that such young children believe that dreams are pictures that are publicly visible and that thinking is overt or covert speech.[4]

Piaget presented cogent illustrations and arguments to reinforce his view. But, Piaget was wrong.* Even three-year-olds can distinguish between a person who owns a dog and one who is thinking about a dog. Contemporary studies have shown that three- and four-year-olds insist that a real, physical dog can be touched, can be seen with the eyes, and can be seen by someone else. But mental entities (a thought about a dog) are not concrete, cannot be seen externally, and are private.

This was such a huge departure from Piaget's iconic views that researchers have studied mental entities in depth,[5] calling for children to make fine distinctions. For instance, a dog that has run away cannot be seen or touched, yet it is still physically real. Maybe children see ideas and thoughts in this same way: They're physical things that are absent, like the runaway dog. Or maybe ideas are physical things but insubstantial ones, like air, smoke, or shadows.

My collaborators and I examined these questions by having preschoolers consider a mental entity (a thought about a dog), a corresponding physical object (a dog), an *absent* physical object (a dog that has run far, far away), and real but intangible things like air, smoke, and shadows. Children judged

---

* Piaget was not wrong about many things he claimed and advocated. He claimed that even young infants thought thoughts, a claim we now know is true, but that was scoffed at in the 1920s when he asserted it. He emphasized that young children discover many things on their own, and they don't need to be instructed about them, something that research on children's theory of mind certainly has confirmed.

whether the entities could be touched or seen with the eyes. Then they were asked to explain their answers.

The children said a mental entity could not be seen or touched. They also said an absent object could not be seen or touched, and that air could not be seen or touched. While these are the answers an adult would give, it's easy to suspect that children don't understand the key differences since they gave the same answers for mental entities and for absent objects. But their explanations show how much they understand.

Children explained (as adults do) that a mental entity—like a thought about a dog—could not be touched because "it's *not* real," "just a dream," "only in his mind." In contrast, they said absent objects, even those far away, were "real" and "solid." Insubstantial physical things like air could not be touched but were nonetheless *real*: "It's real, not pretend." Even three-year-olds understood these differences.

When children say mental entities cannot be touched or are not real, they often explain this by saying they are "inside"—in a person's head or mind. Again, adults say similar things. But what if children mean "inside" literally, for example, the way a swallowed raisin is in the stomach. The raisin is a real physical object, but when it's inside the abdomen, it can no longer be touched or seen. Do young children (as Piaget said) think that thoughts are "in the head" in a real, physical sense?

No. In another set of studies, we had children consider a person (Joe) who swallowed a raisin versus a person (John) who was thinking of a raisin. Even three-year-olds said, "Yes," there *really* is a raisin inside Joe (the swallower) and, "Yes," if a doctor looked inside Joe with a special machine, he would see a raisin inside.

In contrast, these children said, "No," there is *not really* a raisin inside of John (the thinker), not even "really inside John's head." They also said, "No," if a doctor looked inside John's head with a special machine, he would *not* see a raisin. Further, in their explanations, the children insisted that mental entities were different from physical ones. "It's not real." "It's not really anything."

Imaginary Companions

This brings us back to imaginary companions. Several authorities, including Piaget, say imaginary companions are a particularly good example of children's inability to separate the imagined from the real.

Dr. Benjamin Spock was one of them. Spock, who died in 1998, was a famous pediatrician who wrote advice books for new parents. His book, *Baby and Child Care*, first published in 1946, continues to be one of the bestsellers of all time. In his 1976 edition, Spock said:

> This is an appropriate time, while we are discussing imaginary companions, to think about how rudimentary small children's grasp of reality is. Small children can't tell the difference between dreaming and waking life. It isn't very clear to them that a television program is only a performance on a screen. What they enjoy, what they want, what they fear, are apt to seem most real. One of the most important jobs that parents have to take on is to teach their children—gradually over the months and years—to distinguish between fantasy and fact.[6]

Undoubtedly, Spock was influenced by Piaget. But, Spock is just as wrong as Piaget was. In fact, as Marjorie Taylor's research, along with others,[7] shows, young children easily distinguish between fantasy and fact, between the mental and the real, between imagined entities and real physical ones.

Further, children who have imaginary companions not only distinguish between mind and reality, but also show other theory-of-mind strengths. In Taylor's research, young children with imaginary companions consistently performed better than their peers on false-belief tests. Recall the change-of-location scenarios like Glenda and the candy box or Mopfana and the mango kernels. Children with imaginary companions on average understand the actors' false beliefs earlier than their peers.

Mixing Mind and Reality—We All Do It

Of course, children's grip on reality can falter. They can be frightened by their dreams, they can mix up a film with reality, and they can let their imaginations run away with them. They don't always perfectly separate mind and world, but neither do adults. Waking from a bad dream, we can be terrified. While the dream isn't real, the emotions it causes are. We seek out horror movies, not because we think they depict real events but because they provoke in us real terror, although without invoking real danger. That creepy fear comes from a film rather than from a walk in a dangerous, dark neighborhood. But it's vivid and emotionally real, and the experience can be cathartic.

Fiction authors, creators of imaginary persons for themselves and others, say their characters can become for them credible entities, surprisingly helpful ones with minds of their own. The author Enid Blyton said:

> I shut my eyes for a few moments, with my portable typewriter on my knee—
> I make my mind blank, and then as clearly as I would see my real children,
> my characters stand before me. I see them in detail—hair, eyes, feet, clothes,
> expression—and I always know their Christian names, but not their surnames.
> I don't know what anyone is going to say or do. Sometimes a character makes
> a joke, a really funny one, that makes me laugh as I type it on the paper—and
> I think, "Well, I couldn't have thought of that myself in a hundred years!"[8]

This is not an adult's break with reality, a confusion between fact and fiction. This is a creative mind at work, creating mental entities that for the duration of the writing are helpful, welcome, imaginary companions. Children's imaginary companions function similarly.

Children's imaginary companions and their ordinary acts of pretending show us our adult minds in simplified form. Their processes are the foundation an author draws on to create worlds and characters so vivid and real they become part of our lives.

Think of Elizabeth Bennet and Mr. Darcy in Jane Austen's classic, *Pride and Prejudice*. Many people feel they have learned as much from them about Regency England as from all their reading of English history. For aficionados, there are websites and clubs where people dress up like Austen characters and simulate Regency behavior and conversation. There is a popular 2013 advice book, *How to Speak Like Jane Austen and Live Like Elizabeth Bennet: Your Guide to Livelier Language and a Lovelier Lifestyle.*[9]

None of this is adult dysfunction or mental breakdown. It is not adult misconstrual of fiction as real life. It is an adult extension of our childhood powers of imaginary play, including children's invention of imaginary companions. It is adult recognition that fiction, at least good, insightful fiction, conveys real-life truth: Elizabeth Bennet can guide you to a lovelier lifestyle. Fictional thinking is a childhood theory-of-mind brainchild that leads to, and reveals, adult insights.

In Sum

By the time children are three, four, and five years of age, they know not only that thoughts and wants lead to actions, but also key things about lying, about secret keeping, and about persuasion. They know that thoughts are things, but not physical things; that thoughts are hidden, unlike overt actions and appearances; that thoughts are not necessarily true. And, they know their beloved imaginary companions are not real. In fact, at a surprisingly young age children know that some thoughts—true beliefs—are meant to reflect the world and thus shape action in the world. But, imaginings are thoughts that are meant to shape events in a different world, a world of fiction.

Mind, in its variety and beauty, suffuses children's everyday worlds as well as their special, imaginary, worlds. This is also true for adults because we are the beneficiaries of our own childhoods.

5

Putting the Theory in Theory of Mind

Twenty years ago, after decades of failed attempts, a computer beat a grand-master at chess for the first time.[1] It was hailed as a coming of age for artificial intelligence (AI). Chess playing is considered a pinnacle of human intelli-gence. That Deep Blue, an intelligent computer, could beat Gary Kasparov must mean that computers were approaching human levels. Soon, they would do other human tasks: translate languages, recognize speech, even master computer theory so they could design still better computers. Sci-fi books and movies like *2001: A Space Odyssey* reinforced belief in this fast-approaching future.

Many of those predictions have come true. With a laptop, you can now use Google Translate to obtain a translation from your language into scores of other languages. With an iPhone, you can ask Siri for directions, dictate a letter, find restaurant recommendations, or reserve tickets. Amazon's Alexa does these chores and others like allowing car owners to start their car and its air conditioning while sitting at the breakfast table.

So, smart technology must already be human-like and must be getting more so. Right?

Well, no. It was only when scientists gave up trying to duplicate human minds that they could create computers able to perform smart human tasks. These "human" tasks are now done using a highly nonhuman method: mas-sive, brute-force computing. It's called *artificial* intelligence for a reason.[2]

Brute-force computing takes advantage of a computer's vast memory and its massive ability to crunch numbers. Before making a chess move, Deep Blue calculated every possible move it might make from its current position, looking at least six to ten moves ahead. It then evaluated those possible moves against the moves made in 700,000 past grandmaster games that it held in its memory. It could do this at a rate of about 200 million chess positions per second. Using those comparisons, it chose the statistically best next move and was eventually able to beat Gary Kasparov.

Language translation is done in a similar way. For decades, computer scientists tried and failed to get computers to translate the way humans do.

Reading Minds. Henry M. Wellman with Karen Lind, Oxford University Press (2020) © Oxford University Press.
DOI: 10.1093/oso/9780190878672.001.0001

Breakthroughs in computer translation came only when they began to rely on the computer's gigantic, nonhuman memory and comparison abilities.

Now, they enter massive amounts of text in its original version and in versions translated by humans. The computer compares the two and links words and phrases from the original language to words and phrases in the foreign language. This is stored in an immense database. When a translation is required, the computer chooses the foreign word or phrase most often associated with the word or phrase that needs translation.

This "data-mining" process explains not only why Google Translate can quickly offer translations into multiple languages, but also why the translations can be peculiar, nonnative, and even inappropriate. This shows up especially if you want to translate idioms ("that was a close call") or nonliteral metaphors ("she was rocked by the news"). This is also the way computer grammar checkers work and why they will annoyingly miscorrect your perfectly good sentence. While your construction may be accurate, statistically you're not using the most common choice. Autocorrection changes your words, at time producing nonsense, embarrassment, misunderstandings.

Data mining involves trolling through massive amounts of information to note relations between one thing and the next. It's used increasingly with "big data," like all those purchases you and others make on Amazon that allow Amazon to send you ads about products tailored to "folks like you."

Compared to computers, humans are poor at this kind of data mining, yet somehow we play masterful chess and accurately translate languages. We also read minds—something computers can't do. We do all this using a completely different method: We develop theories, particularly a theory of mind. We create an overarching theory to explain the facts and then use our theory to make sense of new details that arise. Or, we alter our theory to accommodate happenings that don't fit. This way of thinking—everyday theoretical thinking—goes far beyond data mining. Temple Grandin gives you a sense of how far beyond.

Temple Grandin: Thinking in Pictures

Temple Grandin told the writer and neurologist Oliver Sacks she has trouble interacting with children. Little children, she feels, already understand other human beings in a way she, as an autistic person, can never do. Children can employ the notions of our theory of mind—thoughts, wants, hopes, ideas, and preferences—to make sense of and appreciate others' lives and minds easily. Grandin, instead, mines data to find the regularities in social interaction.

Grandin explained that, over time, she has built up a vast library of experiences that she stores like videotapes or YouTube clips. She plays these clips in her mind again and again to see how people have behaved in various situations. Then she uses this information to predict how a person in a similar situation might act or how she, in that situation, should act. "It is a strictly logical process," she has said. It's data mining, a taxing process that requires loading her memory with many facts most of us can ignore. And still she misses insights most of us would see easily.

When Grandin's first animal facility kept breaking down, she tracked scores of possible problems before she realized one employee was sabotaging her efforts. Human malfeasance wasn't, to her, logical behavior, and it was foreign to her fact-based mindset. She had to reevaluate her clips from a completely new aspect so she could "learn to be suspicious."

That's life without theory of mind; it's social understanding via data mining. Deep Blue would experience the same problem. It doesn't know that a chess gambit is an attempt to deceive the other player. A gambit is like a ploy, bluff, or scam; it's an interaction meant to create confusion or false beliefs. Deep Blue couldn't set out to confuse. It could only store past examples of chess masters using the Scotch, Queens, or Cochrane gambit and then make that move when it had the best statistical chance of working.

As you can see, Grandin has notions about how minds work generally and ideas about how her mind works particularly. She says her mind operates in concrete pictures; it stores videos and crunches numbers. It's not clear if this description actually captures what her mind does, of course. For example, in her second autobiographical work, *Thinking in Pictures*, she said that people with autism think in pictures, which accounts for both their mental strengths and their social weaknesses.[3] That is incorrect; some individuals with autism often think in pictures, but on average those with autism are no better, and can be worse, than most of us at pictorial thinking. Still, two points remain. First, that *is* her description of her own mind, and, second, that does not describe *our* everyday mental workings when we think about people. She described data mining the social world, not developing a think–want theory.

Walking at night with Oliver Sacks, Grandin said, "When I look up at the stars at night I know I should get a 'numinous' feeling, but I don't. I would like to get it. I can understand it intellectually."

Sacks asked, "Do you get a feeling of its grandeur?"

"I *intellectually* understand its grandeur," she replied. She knows—via data mining—how the term *grand* is applied: to starry nights, to Beethoven sonatas, to ancient ruins. But the feeling, for her, is missing.

This is not an issue of lacking emotion or of having an atypical emotional circuit in her brain. Grandin experiences basic emotions like sadness, anger, and even love. She loves cows. Grandeur, however, is not a basic, raw emotion; it is feeling coupled with mind. It is surprise, but surprise that exists because we are struck, overwhelmed, in touch with mysteries and meanings larger than ourselves.

Grandin has achieved an impressive intellectual understanding of this feeling, but it is not the result that most of us, even children, achieve without a fraction of Grandin's enormous effort. Our "getting it" stems from the way we use and develop our theory of mind. And Grandin, like others with autism, does not have our common theory of mind and so misses out on this ordinary childhood achievement.

Everyday Theories

Grandin's differences help us understand how we form our everyday theories, especially our theory of mind. The process is very like the way scientists develop theories. Scientists accumulate data through observations or experiments. But, they do more than attempt to detect regularities in that data. They try to understand and explain why it is this way and not some other way. Stephen Hawking, the famous theoretical physicist, said, "Science is beautiful when it makes simple explanations of phenomena."[4] We are all trying to make this kind of beauty.

Scientists use theories to help them explain and understand what's going on. Their theories allow them to organize and simplify complex raw phenomena. They can use the theory instead of individual facts and correlations to chart connections between different observations. Then, they can organize multiple constructs into larger systems--theories like Einstein's relativity or Darwin's evolution. A theory can also be used to make predictions: What will new data look like when we collect that?

Complicated as this process sounds, we all build theories every day. You're sitting at a restaurant alone, at a table for two. Your date—Stacy—has not appeared, and not appeared, and not appeared. You think, "I bet he forgot."

After all, your larger theory of mind tells you people often forget; memory is fallible. You also consider your theory about Stacy himself. Stacy's is generally conscientious, but lately he's been distracted, and his cell phone has been on the blink, so maybe he couldn't check his calendar or call you. Your best explanation is that his failure to show is an unusual occurrence but completely understandable. It makes sense because of the interplay between your overall theory of mind and your specific theory about Stacy's mind and behavior—case solved.

But the next day when you call Stacy, he is not apologetic, refuses a new date, changes the subject, and cuts the call short. Then, he doesn't answer his phone or return your calls for several more days. You must rethink what just happened. Your theory of mind gives you a new explanation: Affections can change and feelings fade. Maybe "it's off" with Stacy.

This is not data mining. You aren't just keeping track of appearances and failed calls and then calculating the trends. You're going beyond the data to interpret it via your theories and constructs. You conclude that Stacy's failure to show was not a statistical anomaly; this is a person doing things he *thinks* will get him what he *wants*. He's breaking it off; you're being dumped. Using your theory, you don't just accumulate the data, you interpret it, quickly and meaningfully.

And your theory—your "Stacy" theory and your "our relationship" theory—develops. It shifts from fallible memory to lost affection based on the data you've accumulated. Your new theory may be wrong, of course. Maybe Stacy had a mild stroke and is temporarily not himself. Theories can lead you astray, but they operate insistently, and they allow for change.

Theory of mind is our worldview. This is true for children, too. They are developing a theory of mind from their very earliest years, a foundation we draw on for the rest of our lives.

Building Theories

As scientific theories change and are revised, they manifest three signature features:

1. Theories change in a progression of steps.
   Theories of astronomy, for example, progressed. The earth is flat → the earth is round → the sun rotates around the round earth → the earth rotates around the massive sun.

2. The changes grow from evidence.

Observations made by seafaring Greeks, then observations made in observatories, and finally observations using telescopes and cameras, helped shift theories of astronomy. New evidence or different sorts of evidence can impede, speed up, or alter progressions.

3. Prior theories constrain and enable later ones.

Understanding the earth was round made it possible for astronomers to think the sun orbits the earth. That notion at first stood in the way of thinking the earth might orbit the sun, but it encouraged more careful observation of the sun, moon, and planets, which enabled different calculations and comparisons. In the end, those calculations led to heliocentrism. Albert Einstein began with Newton's theory and transformed it. Stephen Hawking began with Einstein's theory and extended it.

Theory? Or Not?

That's also how our theory of mind works because it really is a theory.

This may sound unlikely. Science is practiced by a small minority and is supported by advanced degrees and advanced technologies. This doesn't apply to everyday thinking. But the similarities are telling. First, the theories we use to understand people, actions, and minds develop from the interplay between data and theory (not data mining) just like scientific theories do.

Second, our theory of mind functions the way a scientific theory does. It gives us a framework we can use to incorporate and make sense of everyday happenings. Scientific and everyday theories work the same way, even though theory of mind is supported by everyday experiences and observations, while scientific theory may be supported by an advanced degree and a telescope.

Understanding everyday theories allows us to make sense of some otherwise-puzzling facts. Science is convincing to us because we recognize the basic value of explaining and predicting what goes on around us. We do it all the time. Also, science and scientific theories developed the way they did because scientists have the same brains as the rest of us. Our basic theory building—as scientists and nonscientists—proceeds from the theory-of-mind skills we learn as babies and young children.

As my colleague Alison Gopnik and I have often claimed, it's not that children are little scientists. That puts the focus on the complexities of science. Instead, it's that scientists are big children who build theories like the rest of us, only they do it using more system and more precision.[5] That comparison puts the focus where it belongs: on children. Stephen Hawking has said, "I am just a child who has never grown up. I still keep asking these 'how' and 'why' questions. Occasionally, I find an answer." Our theory building provides some of our most impressive, distinctively human, forms of learning and understanding.*

The differences between science and everyday life, and between scientific theories and everyday theories, are real. But the similarities are also real. They point to the genesis of all theories from human understanding and, more specifically, their genesis from human social understanding. Science is a social enterprise. It requires collaboration; it requires sensitivity to what others believe; and it requires knowledge of how to persuade others with belief-based evidence. These are all tasks that most four-year-olds can perform. It requires building on prior knowledge and generating hypotheses based on evidence, which children also do. It places a premium on explanation, something young children spark with their "Why?" "Why?" "Why?" questions. Our complex scientific theories require cognitive and social skills that are born and grow as children achieve their theory of minds.

If theorizing really explains how children accumulate their ideas, then children's theories of mind should show the same three signature features as scientific theories:

1. Developing theories of mind should unfold in a progression of steps.
2. The changes should grow from evidence, so different experiences can yield different timetables and sequences of understanding.
3. Prior knowledge should constrain, and enable, later learning.

Let's see.

---

* Of course, we build theories in many areas. Temple Grandin is able to build theories when she designs animal facilities. She gathers data, weighs possibilities against facts, and reaches a conclusion about the best design for the cattle and their owners. But, she can't apply this same method to understanding her fellow humans' psychology, a skill easily learned by the nonautistic.

6

Block by Block

Mallie was a beautiful baby with dark curly hair, large dark eyes, and a cherubic square face. Mallie's parents, first timers Joe and Ellen, brought her home from the hospital with joy and fanfare, making plans for her future: a soccer star, a PhD scientist, president of the United States.

She was an easy, responsive baby, babbling and cooing, and lighting up when Ellen played "This Little Piggy" or Joe blew raspberries on her round belly. Joe and Ellen were convinced she was the most wonderful baby on the planet—maybe she was.

Mallie was more than a year old when Ellen first became concerned. Her babbling had fallen off, and she had not yet spoken a word.

"The service is too good," Joe said. "She doesn't have to talk. And there's nothing wrong with her brain. She can make all the baby signs* we've taught her, and she's made up some of her own."

But Ellen couldn't relax. Mallie seemed less responsive than other kids her age—fine when they interacted face to face, but in her own world sometimes and impossible to engage if you weren't right with her.

Mallie was two when her pediatrician referred her to a hearing specialist, and it was a month more before she was diagnosed as profoundly deaf, probably from birth.

Mallie's experience is not uncommon for deaf children born to hearing parents because deafness is harder to diagnose than it might seem. Most deaf children, like Mallie, babble and interact. They also startle to loud noises. Loud sounds set off shock waves as well as sound waves, and deaf children react to them. Or, they can feel vibrations from something like a loud bass speaker playing nearby. The differences between hearing and deaf babies can be subtle; parents, and even pediatricians, regularly miss them. And at the

---

* Many parents now use simplified sign gestures with their young preverbal children, termed *baby signs* by their inventor Linda Acredolo at the University of California–Davis. Common ones are those for "more," "milk," "no more," and "all gone." When children begin using verbal words a few months later, baby signs typically fall away from disuse.

Reading Minds. Henry M. Wellman with Karen Lind, Oxford University Press (2020) © Oxford University Press.
DOI: 10.1093/oso/9780190878672.001.0001

time Mallie was born, not all newborns in the United States were routinely given a hearing test.*

After the diagnosis, Joe and Ellen went through shock, denial, grief, and anger. They had to drastically rearrange their ideas about Mallie's childhood, their participation in that childhood, and her future. Only then could they begin to learn how to best parent Mallie. It was a slow process because, like most U.S. adults, they knew little about deafness and still less about education, services, and opportunities for deaf children.

When Mallie turned three, Ellen took on the herculean task of learning American Sign Language (ASL). It would help Mallie's language learning, as well as her later educational achievements like reading. And, the earlier they started, the better.

Of course, Mallie and her parents were already communicating. They pointed to objects, played finger games, waved bye-bye. They used some baby signs, and they had unconsciously developed some "home sign," gestures they all understood, such as finger waggles for "tickle," chest patting for "me," and head patting for "hat" or "hair." And Mallie, more than her parents, would put two home signs together in a regular order to express larger thoughts and requests, like "tickle me," and "Mommy hat."

So, Mallie and her mom had a place to start. But ASL, like other sign languages and like spoken language, is complex and arbitrary. The spoken word for "mom," "house," or "name" has no real relation to a mother, a house, or someone's name, and the same holds true for ASL signs. Further, ASL has its own grammar and syntax, which is unlike English and unlike any spoken language. It uses space and three dimensions instead of words in a sequence.

Despite her resolute efforts to learn ASL, Ellen never achieved real proficiency. Hearing parents rarely do, especially in a child's early years. Ellen signed the way a beginning speaker with phrase-book Spanish might speak, using simple signs or gestures to refer to here-and-now objects.

Recognizing her limitations—she wasn't going to be good at ASL grammar and syntax—Ellen focused on what she could do. She taught Mallie signs for common, visible objects and actions: book, girl, ball, dog, run, drink, spoon. Unlike most hearing parents (and unlike deaf parents of deaf children), most of her interactions with Mallie were spent teaching.[1]

---

* By 2010, all states had some requirement for screening newborn hearing, but nationwide the practice is inconsistent. Even today, about 5% of US newborns aren't screened.

Ellen and Joe worked valiantly, but Mallie's experience was vastly different from that of a deaf child born to deaf parents. Those deaf children become "native signers." From birth, other native signers around a deaf child surround them with sentences that naturally become more complex as the child grows older, just like hearing parents do with hearing children. And the adults around native signing children communicate with each other in a form the child can access: visually. These deaf children grow up in an environment that is intensely interactive and free flowing, in a way they can understand, from birth. Mallie's interactions, in comparison, were segmented and didactic.

Once Mallie started school, she interacted daily with other deaf children, some of whom were native signers, and with sign-fluent teachers. Consequently, her sign language quickly outpaced Ellen's. Her community both expanded beyond her family and narrowed—she more and more preferred to interact with signers.

Building Theory of Mind

Because of differences in their interaction, socialization, and communication, Mallie and other deaf children differ enormously from hearing children in the speed of their theory-of-mind development, and that significantly impacts their futures. Of course deafness is only one of numerous childhood experiences that can influence theory-of-mind development, but it is a profound one.

Theory of mind is a complex edifice of ideas about peoples' mental lives. It rests on and gives rise to thinking about intentions, thoughts, emotions, imagination, mental entities, and the privacy of mind. These are the sources of our propensity to pretend, deceive, understand, persuade, and teach.

The result is a towering achievement. But like any complex construction project, it must proceed in steps, over time. Researchers have discovered they can track a child's progress through these steps by focusing on a few key milestones:

1. *Diverse Desires*: People can have different preferences, even for the same things. When a child understands this, he or she would understand, for example, one person likes apples while another does not.
2. *Diverse Beliefs*: People can have different beliefs about the same situation. Suppose a child sees two people considering a plain, closed box.

When a child reaches this milestone, he or she would understand that each of them could have a different idea about the contents. More generally, the child would understand that beliefs can differ from one person to another.

3. *Knowledge–Ignorance*: Besides just having different beliefs, someone may actually know what is in the box (an apple!), while someone else could not know but instead be ignorant. A child would understand that difference, or generally, the child would understand that some people can be ignorant of what others know.

4. *False Belief*: Being ignorant is different from having a false belief. In *Romeo and Juliet*, Romeo isn't just ignorant about what happened to Juliet, he *thinks* (falsely) she is dead. In achieving this milestone, a child would understand that an event may be true but someone could believe something totally false about it.

5. *Hidden Minds*: All these internal states—wants, knowledge, ignorance, and thoughts—are not necessarily visible in a person's actions or expressions. Someone who hates apples may pretend to like them to be courteous to a host; someone who is ignorant may make a lucky guess and appear to know. Children come to understand: Minds can be hidden.

Figure 6.1 illustrates these steps.

These cartoon-like depictions show the steps a child takes toward understanding people's mental states. Researchers have explored each of these steps in depth. One of my favorite studies, the first of the now-classic broccoli-goldfish studies, looked at the first step, Diverse Desires.

Betty Repacholi and Alison Gopnik at the University of California-Berkeley asked eighteen-month-olds to taste broccoli and goldfish crackers and to tell the researchers which they preferred.[2] Not surprisingly, almost all the children chose goldfish crackers. Then Betty faced the child and tasted each snack. She said, "Yum" and smiled for one snack, and said, "Yuck," and frowned for the other. About half the children watched her do this in a *Match* situation: She liked the crackers (yum) and disliked the broccoli (yuck), which matched the child's preference. For the other half, Betty provided a *Mismatch*: She liked the broccoli and didn't like the crackers.

Now came the test. Two small bowls were placed on the table between Betty and the child. One held goldfish crackers; the other held broccoli florets. Betty held her hand halfway between the two bowls, looked at the child, and said, "I want some more, can you give me some more?"

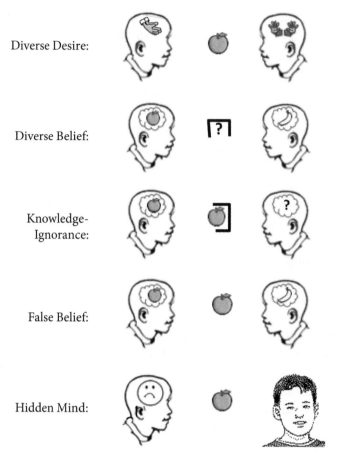

Diverse Desire:

Diverse Belief:

Knowledge-
Ignorance:

False Belief:

Hidden Mind:

These cartoon-like depictions show the steps a child
takes toward understanding people's mental states.

Figure 6.1 Steps toward theory-of-mind understanding.

Although Betty carefully avoided indicating either bowl, the eighteen-
month-olds overwhelmingly gave Betty the snack she had said she liked. In
the *Mismatch* situation, this meant they gave Betty broccoli; in the *Match* situation, they gave her crackers.

The broccoli–goldfish test shows that children understand *Diverse
Desires*: Different people have different wants, urges, and avoidances. While
the child might like goldfish, Betty likes broccoli. Slightly older children can
explain this clearly:

ROSS (AGE THREE AND A HALF): This, what I got on my bread, was sour on my
tongue. . . . I don't like it. [Hands bread to his father]
FATHER: What makes you think that Daddy's going to like it?
ROSS: Because you like sour stuff. So eat it.

Stepping Up

The distinctions made in these five steps may seem overly detailed. Kids will get to theory-of-mind understanding without our knowing the details. But as you saw in Chapter 3, details about when children become competent at theory-of-mind understanding can affect their lives far into the future.

Researchers have tested hundreds of preschoolers in the United States, Canada, Australia, Germany, and other countries on their understanding of the five steps in this Theory-of-Mind Scale.[3] As Figure 6.2 shows, children learn the steps going up the stairs from left to right, in order. If a young child knows only one thing, it's Diverse Desires. If a child knows three things, it's Diverse Desires, Diverse Beliefs, and Knowledge–Ignorance. Children don't master skills on the right of the figure (False Beliefs, say) before they master the steps to the left of them.

So, theory-of mind learning follows the first signature feature of general theory learning outlined in Chapter 5: **Theories of mind change in a progression of steps**.

We also have determined the average age when children master a task—numbers that hold true in numerous Western nations. Figure 6.2 shows that most children master all five steps by five-and-a-half years of age.

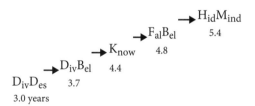

Figure 6.2 The stair-step pattern of theory-of-mind understanding. Div_{Des} = Diverse Desires; Div_{Bel} = Diverse Beliefs; Know = Knowledge–Ignorance; FalBel = False Belief; HidMind = Hidden Mind. The numbers (e.g., 3.7 years) show the average age (in years) at which children understand each step.

But, theory-of-mind development can be delayed. Profoundly deaf children of hearing parents, like Mallie, experience severe delays in theory-of-mind development. Their delays can be as long as delays for children with autism, although the causes are completely different.

Figure 6.3 shows children's progress on the Theory-of-Mind Scale, but separates deaf and hearing children. Deaf children of hearing parents proceed up the scale in the same order as hearing kids do, but they learn each step later.

Deaf Children with Deaf Parents

Understanding is vastly different for the 5 percent of deaf children who have one or more deaf parents. Like hearing children, they are bathed in language and social communication from an early age. The only difference is that this happens in sign not speech. *Native signers* rise step by step on the Theory-of-Mind Scale on exactly the same timetable as the hearing children, as shown in Figure 6.3.

The other 95 percent of deaf children can't access language because it's spoken. If they learn sign language, like Mallie did, they learn it later in life. They're called *late signers*. Their theory-of-mind delays are severe and extend through their early adolescence and even into adulthood. And, as we've seen, even mild delays in a child's theory of mind can influence the child's

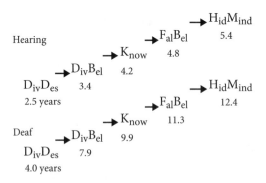

Figure 6.3 Theory of mind understanding for hearing children and for deaf children of hearing parents. Just as in Figure 6.2, Div_{Des} = Diverse Desires; Div_{Bel} = Diverse Beliefs; Know = Knowledge–Ignorance, and so on. The numbers show the average age at which children understand each step.

acquisition of social skills, social interactions with peers, and transition to school.

Deaf children show us that theory of mind is learned, not innate. It doesn't happen inevitably or deaf children of hearing parents would be on the same timetable as hearing kids. The deaf community in Nicaragua reinforces this conclusion.

Watching a Sign Language Arise

Sign languages are not like the pantomimes and gestures we use in playing charades or like the Native American sign system that was developed for trade between tribes. They are complete languages that use grammar and sentence structures as complex as those of spoken languages. And, they are as different from one another as Spanish is from Chinese and Chinese is from English. In fact, the distinctions in sign are even wider. While speakers in the United States, Australia, and Britain understand each other, people who use ASL, Australian Sign Language (Auslan), and British Sign Language (BSL) can't communicate.

Sign languages develop when communities of deaf people live together and interact over multiple generations. Until recently, Nicaragua had no sign language because deaf people lived in isolation. Most often, a single deaf person would live in a small rural community. But in 1979 the Sandinistas took over Nicaragua and reformed the education system. Among other changes, they created a school for the deaf in Managua, which many deaf children from around the country attended.

The school taught using a strict "oralist" method. It focused on drilling children in lip reading and mouth exercises to try to teach spoken words. Classes were taught by hearing, not deaf, speakers. Historically, this has been the primary approach to deaf education. Uniformly, the results have been dismal, as they were in Nicaragua.

But, on the buses and playgrounds and at lunchtime, children gestured to each other to communicate. The first cohort of students—those who arrived in the first two or three years of the school's existence—created only a crude gestural system, like Native American sign language.

When the second cohort arrived a few years later, they were exposed to the initial gestural system, *and* they improved on it. They added tenses to verbs and modifiers to nouns, and they used longer and longer sentence-like strings. They made the system more complex and more complete.

The third cohort, who arrived a few years later still, improved the language even further to develop what became known as Idioma de Signos Nicaraguense (ISL). ISL was the collective product of a community of deaf students interacting with each other over successive cohorts.

In learning any language—spoken or signed—there is a critical period for becoming fluent. Unless you are exposed to a language early enough, you will always speak accented, incomplete, phrase-book Spanish or Chinese.*

This is what happened to the first cohort of ISL signers, who learned sign language in their teens. They were, essentially, nonnative, simplistic users of a truncated gestural system. Their signing was mostly about here-and-now events: The words for "cat," "run," or "home" were stitched together in simple phrases like "cat run home." This first-generation ISL, and its speakers, had few words for nonobservable things and none for a person's mental states (their desires, ideas, or minds), words like "think" and "want."

That changed over successive cohorts. By the third cohort, younger speakers had advanced the language so that today ISL is fully formed. Speakers have a full set of words and language structures, including mental state words.[4]

Fortunately for us, a longitudinal study was conducted with the first cohort of ISL users: those who grew up without the words or grammar to express mental states. When this first cohort was tested at about age twenty-two, most could not pass standard false-belief tests. (That is, they had not mastered even the fourth level on the Theory-of-Mind Scale, a test that hearing Nicaraguan children master by age five.)

However, over the next several years, these adults joined a deaf social club. They learned signs for mental states by conversing with the younger deaf cohort who had grown up using them. The sophistication of their grammar didn't change, but their vocabulary did. When tested again at about age twenty-five, the false-belief performance of this older, first cohort had improved until it rivaled that of the younger cohort.

Timetables for theory-of-mind learning depend on the experiences children undergo, and they can be seriously delayed. Fortunately for children with delays, theory-of-mind learning can continue well into adulthood.

---

* Only very rare individuals can come to speak like "natives" as adults.

Enhancing Theory of Mind

Clearly, an adverse situation can cause theory-of-mind delays, with all their negative consequences. Can an enhanced situation speed up or improve theory-of-mind development? That also could have consequences, but of a positive sort.

Jennifer Amsterlaw, Marjorie Rhodes, and I decided to find out by focusing on one key milestone: understanding False Beliefs. In several studies,[5] we looked at young three-year-olds, all of whom systematically failed false-belief tests. Half of these children were assigned to a baseline group where nothing in their environment changed. Because children this age ordinarily require from one to three years to move from consistent false-belief error to consistent correct performance, it was no surprise that children in this baseline group showed virtually no progress in false-belief understanding in the twelve weeks of the study.

The children in the target experimental group were given enhanced experiences. In multiple sessions over six weeks, these children saw dozens of different false-belief skits: Max looks for his hidden candy; Sarah puts her favorite doll in the playroom, but it gets moved to the bedroom when she's not looking; Jose's dog escapes and hides in the garage; and others. After each skit, the children were asked to predict where the searcher would look for the hidden object.

Initially, these children, who had consistently failed false-belief tests in a pretest, predicted wrongly. They said, for example, that Sara would look for her doll in the bedroom where it really was, even though Sara had put her doll in the playroom and hadn't seen it moved.

After their predictions, the children saw Sara go to the playroom, not the bedroom, to find her doll. Then they were asked, "Why did Sara do that?" Whatever the child answered, the researcher replied, "Oh, thanks."

Initially, the children's explanations of Sara's behavior were weak and off track. They might say something irrelevant about her desires: "She changed; now she doesn't like that doll." Or just, "I don't know."

But over the days and sessions, the children's explanations improved. They began to say things like, "She didn't see her doll was moved," or, "She doesn't know her doll's not there," or even, "She thinks her doll is in the playroom." And this happened even though children never received feedback on their explanations beyond, "Oh, thanks."

False-belief predictions improved along with the children's explanations. Their predictions went from essentially 0 percent correct to about 70 percent correct by the end of the twelve sessions.

We learned that children's theory-of-mind reasoning can be improved and how it could be done. Requiring children to make predictions followed by explanations gave them more chances to create and explain theories. It engaged them in theory building, and that sparked theory-of-mind advances (Sidebar 6.1).

These studies, added to the deaf child data, underwrite the timetable part of the second signature piece about theory-based learning: **Theory of mind**

Sidebar 6.1 Why the Why?

In our studies, we concentrated on having children explain things. Young children are fascinated by why things happen. That's why most preschoolers go through a period when they ask "Why?" "Why?" "Why?" sometimes driving parents batty.

> CHILD (3 years, 9 months): Can you eat snails?
> MOTHER: Yes, some people eat snails.
> CHILD: Why?
> MOTHER: Because they like them.
> CHILD: Why? . . . I don't like to eat snails. . . .
> Why do some people like snails?

And, the topic children most want to know about is why people do what they do (they eat snails?!?).

Helpful experiences can speed up children's theory-of-mind development, and the lack of these experiences can slow that development. A helpful experience of the first magnitude is when a child has to explain things. That encourages theory creation and revision. In fact, in correlational research, children who do more explaining in conversations with their parents at home perform best on false-belief tests in the laboratory.

Children, like adults, create theories to make predictions and to explain why things happen. Their predictions fail, so they wrestle with the failures to find a better explanation of what is going on. From these experiences they form a revised theory. That is what we had them do in our studies.

changes grow from evidence, so different experiences can yield different timetables and sequences of understanding.

Can Sequences Differ?

So far, the discussion has concerned timetables. What about sequences? If theory of mind is learned from experiences, then different experiences might alter children's steps through the sequences. A natural experiment, one that compares children who grow up in Western versus Chinese cultures, sheds light on this conjecture.

Researchers say that Western and Asian cultures differ dramatically in terms of individualism versus collectivism. People in the West focus on individuality and independence. People in China hold a prevalent Asian focus on group commonalities and interdependence. Historians trace these differences back as far as Aristotle, who focused on truth, subjectivity, and belief; and Confucius, who focused more on pragmatic and consensual knowledge that all right-minded people should learn.

In their conversations with young children about people, Chinese parents comment on "knowing" who has correct or good knowledge and who does not. In the United States, parents comment more on "thinking" and on the differences between various individuals' ideas and thoughts.

In line with these differences, Chinese preschoolers consistently show a different theory-of-mind sequence on the Theory-of-Mind Scale. Figure 6.4 compares children in the United States and Australia with children growing up in Beijing, China. Both Western and Chinese children first understand

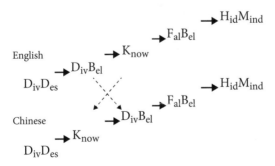

Figure 6.4 Sequence of theory-of-mind learning: Comparing Beijing to English-speaking US and Australian preschoolers.

Diverse Desires, but after that Western children learn Diverse Beliefs, whereas Chinese children next learn Knowledge–Ignorance.* Step 2 and Step 3 are reversed.

Comparisons like these show that children may step up through theory-of-mind understandings differently in different places.[6] Although, in the end, most children arrive at a set of "standard" insights and skills for reading minds, the sequence of their acquisition is shaped by cultural differences.

These further studies reinforce the second signature feature of theory learning: **Changes grow from evidence, so different experiences can yield different timetables *and* sequences of understanding.** Theory-of-mind timetables and sequences both depend on children's social and communication experiences.

Theories Beget Theories

What about the third feature of theory-based learning? **Prior theories constrain and enable later ones.**

In our theory-of-mind training sessions, the children, on average, improved, but their range of achievement varied widely. By the posttest, some children were 100 percent correct on false-belief tasks, some were 50 percent correct, and some remained largely incorrect. Yet, all these children were exposed to the same experiences. Why were their outcomes so different?

In some of our studies, we gave children initial tests to find out where they fell on the Theory-of-Mind Scale. At pretest, all the children in our study consistently failed false-belief tests (Step 4). But, about half understood Knowledge–Ignorance (Step 3), while half had gotten only as far as Diverse Beliefs (Step 2). So, some started the experiment further along the theory-of-mind progression than others.

Of the children who had reached Step 3 (Knowledge–Ignorance), 75 percent consistently passed false-belief tests at the end of the study. Of those who had reached only Step 2 (Diverse Beliefs), none consistently passed false-belief tests.

Children's progress depended on their experiences because only those children with training progressed. But, it also depended on what a child

---

* This is not a singular peculiarity of the Chinese mind and development. Children in Iran, another collectivist culture, show the same alternative sequence, where understanding Knowledge–Ignorance precedes understanding Diverse Beliefs.

understood when training began. Most children who began at Step 3 came to understand false beliefs, while most children who started at Step 2 did not.

This is evidence for the third signature piece: A child's progress depends not only on his formative experiences, but also on his initial theories. When children were closer to understanding false belief, it enabled learning; they really improved. When further away, it constrained learning.

Building with Blocks

Childhood learning is not just gathering knowledge, and it's not finding trends—mining data. It is most like a scientist building new theories off earlier ones. Copernicus built off Ptolemy by using new data, then Galileo built off Copernicus. Children build their theories of mind on their earlier understandings and experiences.

Children's early understanding of wants gives them a way to understand people and their behaviors. Dad really likes donuts, so he goes to the cupboard to get one. But, what if he looks somewhere else, like the refrigerator? You and I easily think, "He doesn't know where the donuts are" (Knowledge–Ignorance). Or, "He thinks they're in the fridge" (False Belief).

For a child who's limited to understanding wants, however, it's a puzzle. Why doesn't Dad go to the cupboard to get donuts? That's what he wants. As the child tries to explain it to themselves, the child learns some new ideas about people. Not only do wants count, but a person's thoughts are important too, and sometimes they're most important.

Do kids really do this, building a theory of mind step by step? It doesn't sound very childlike. Yet, we watch children build towers with blocks, placing bigger blocks on the bottom to support others on top. Or, we see them watch a tower topple and then revise what they do next to get a better, higher tower. Block building is one of the tasks used on almost all IQ tests for preschool children: Higher towers of increased complexity require and reveal advancing intelligence in the preschool years.

Assembling a theory of mind happens less visibly, but it happens in much the same way: through explorations, discovery, and in steps. In this case, the child uses cognitive blocks and a cognitive assembly of ideas. This process, which was at first mysterious to child researchers, has always been as much child's play to children as their building with physical blocks.

Theory of mind is an edifice built in steps, and those steps not only illuminate its nature, but also show us what is needed for progress. Children must learn to build and alter theories. It is a monumental achievement of childhood that allows us to read minds as adults. It's a gift our younger selves pass on to us—a skill we use and continue to develop through the rest of our lives.

7

The Baby Boom

Where Reading Minds Begins

Reading Minds begins with preschoolers because they establish a way station. Their accomplishments are the destination for earlier learning and the departure point for learning to come. But preschool understanding itself springs from an infant launch pad.

Message number one in this chapter is that babies are not the mindless beings scientists once thought them. Even in the first year of infancy, they have remarkable knowledge about their social worlds. They may be small, but they are not small-minded. Message number two? This knowledge is not something babies gain innately. Instead, among their innate abilities is an extraordinary predisposition to learn, especially about their social worlds.

Before age two, the end of infancy, children have a foundation for all the social development that is to come, setting the stage for the massive growth in social understanding we see in preschoolers. Like their preschool siblings, infants learn by careful observation and by putting pieces together, like assembling blocks in a tower.

For years no one really knew this. How could we? These tiny people can't talk and have limited physical control. It's taken years of investigative ingenuity to discover how clever babies are. The story of how researchers have uncovered what infants understand is almost as amazing as the discoveries that have emerged.

Infants' Social Understanding

Long before researchers caught up, parents would say their children had social understanding from a very early age. My first moment came when Trey was only a few months old. I looked at a bird, and Trey turned his head to look, too. Then, he looked back at me and smiled.

Reading Minds. Henry M. Wellman with Karen Lind, Oxford University Press (2020) © Oxford University Press.
DOI: 10.1093/oso/9780190878672.001.0001

"Ah," I thought, "Trey and I are sharing an interest." He was telling me, "You like it, and so do I."

Was this true? Or was this my mind reading going full blast, attributing to Trey thoughts, emotions, and desires that didn't exist in a child so young just because I wanted them to be there? Can a baby understand another person's likes? Isn't it more reasonable to assume that an infant's looks and smiles are automatically triggered because of some unknown instinctive agenda.

For decades, this was the scientific consensus, despite parents' assertions. An infant's world is a "blooming, buzzing confusion," said William James, the father of academic psychology, in 1890. Events parade across a baby's senses, tugging the baby's attention in a meaningless dance, James and many others believed. No one suggested any organizing principle like a theory of mind.

So, did Trey have any awareness of my likes or of our sharing an experience? Or was this just my view through the rose-tinted glasses of parenthood? What *do* babies think about people? And how could scientists possibly find out?

How It's Done

Historically, we have very little written information about children's social understanding. Mothers', grandmothers', and midwives' vast practical knowledge was transferred only by word of mouth. Diaries provided some more lasting information: daily notes from a parent about one or two babies growing up over time. But these weren't systematic or comprehensive; they focused on what a parent noticed on one day or another. Or, they focused on one narrow slice of an infant's progress: the baby's first words or motor milestones like rolling over, sitting, crawling, and walking. That was the case until one set of diaries, published by Jean Piaget in the 1930s, became hugely influential. It was both remarkably systematic and widely comprehensive.

Piaget's diaries provided hour after hour of detailed, specific, skillfully organized, and highly insightful recordings about his three children over the first years of their lives.[1] These were handwritten and recorded on paper; Piaget had no recording devices or computers to make his job easier. On reading these exhaustive notes, it seems impossible they could have been the work of one person—and they weren't. Many of the notes were recorded by Piaget's wife, Valentine, herself a trained scientist who remained at home with the children while Piaget was at the university. We know this from historical sleuthing; Piaget himself never mentioned his wife's authorship. The diaries remain a landmark scientific effort, insightful and worth reading to this day, but the work of two observers not just one.

Preferences

Piaget concluded that even newborns have definite visual and auditory preferences. We now know their preferences often focus on sights and sounds from people. Why does this matter? Increased attention to the landscape of people jumpstarts a life of social learning. A social focus gives an enormous boost to an organism—a young human—that needs to make sense of its social world to survive.

It took decades after Piaget's observations for scientists to find methods that could document that babies did, in fact, focus on the world of people. In 1961, at his university in Cleveland, Robert Fantz first systematically measured babies' visual attention.[2] Fantz showed babies a sign that had a line drawing of a face on one half and a bullseye on the other half. The sign had a peephole in it. Fantz hid behind the sign and peered through the peephole to watch where the infants looked.

Fantz discovered that two-month-old babies looked twice as long at the face as they did at the bullseye. Then, he questioned: Did babies prefer faces, or were they just interested in the more complex picture?

Fantz refined his method so babies looked at a picture of a face alongside another picture that was equally complex. Still, hands down, infants looked at the human face. He went on to determine that infants are even more discriminating than that. At just a few weeks of age, an infant would rather look at a picture of his mother's face than at a picture of another woman's face whose hair was a similar length and color.

Other researchers made a further discovery. Babies also showed their preferences by how much and how hard they sucked. Infants suck more and harder when they're hungry. But when they're not hungry, they still like to suck, and they suck more and harder when they look at or hear something that interests them.

Using pacifiers developed to automatically record sucking, researchers have found that infants' attention to sounds, like their attention to sights, are also social. Babies only a few days old suck more when they hear their mother's voice than when they hear a stranger's voice or a random noise.

Further research showed babies would rather listen to their mother's voice than to any other sound in the world.[3]

For babies to register this sort of attention requires more effort than you might think. Sucking takes work, and sucking harder takes more work. Young babies will work harder—suck still more vigorously if needed—to continue listening to their mother's voice.

Obviously these findings can't show us what infants think, only where they attend. We can't say, for example, that Sammie "likes" his Mom's voice better than another, only that he attends more to it and does so even if it takes work. Regardless, this ability to direct their primary focus on humans probably helped Sammie's forebears survive, and it helps Sammie learn.

Once scientists realized they could determine what babies attended to, they wanted to know: Can babies make any sense of the social information they take in? That's what would show us the first beginnings of the theory of mind that will blossom in preschoolers.

Here, also, finding a method at first seemed insurmountable. Babies have such a limited range: no words, few deliberate gestures. It took until the 1980s for researchers to crack the code. The new methodology exploited the fact that babies become bored if they see the same thing too often. When they do, the infant begins to look away. Show Susie the same picture of Mom again and again, and eventually she'll get bored and look elsewhere. If you then change the picture to show her a stranger, she'll look longer at the stranger, even though ordinarily she would rather look at Mom. She recognizes the stranger as new, and a bored infant prefers to look at something new.

This method asks the baby a question with a yes or no response: "Is this new to you?" If the child attends more, the answer is yes. If the child doesn't, the answer is no. Infant researchers then used the babies' responses, called a violation of expectation, to dig deeper. Yes-or-no questions were strung together in a series to learn what infants think.

I first saw this in action in Elizabeth Spelke's laboratory. Spelke is a deservedly famous infant researcher at Harvard. She pioneered violation-of-expectation methods and along the way radically changed our understanding of human cognition. Her research laboratory is a beehive of research assistants simultaneously conducting multiple studies on different aspects of infant cognition.[4] Spelke, who is affectionately called the "baby lady," presides. It was in her laboratory that I learned how to do infant research. The procedures we use in my Infant Cognition Project (also known as the "Baby Lab") at Michigan are directly inspired by hers, as is the way we recruit parents to bring their babies to the laboratory, the way we train student assistants, and more.

Spelke's work, until very recently, centered on what babies think about the physical world of balls, walls, tables, and rattles. I wanted to know what babies think about the social world of people and minds.*

How Infants Understand People

When you first hear the phrase, "what babies think about people," it can sound unlikely. Babies think? Even in their very first months of life? Aren't they really just looking around, sometimes attentive and sometimes bored? Again, how could we gather scientific evidence to decide?

In the 1990s, Amanda Woodward, a postdoctoral alumna of Spelke's, moved from Harvard to the University of Chicago and began to use the violation-of-expectation method to look at what infants understand about people.[5] Woodward, a petite dynamo, and her team of assistants, enacted a short skit for babies less than four months old. Susie sees a man sitting between two objects: a toy frog on an orange mat to his right and a toy duck on a purple mat to his left. The man looks at Susie and says, "Hey, Susie." Then he reaches right and grasps, but doesn't move, the frog. An assistant measures how long Susie looks at that frozen tableau before she looks away. The same skit is performed again and again until Susie barely glances at the scene before looking away.

The question Woodward asked is: How does the baby register this skit? Does Susie see it merely as a repetitive movement, or has the baby gone further? Does she think, "That man wants that frog." Woodward's next skits—the test events--answered those questions.

While Susie is not looking, the position of the objects is switched. For half the Susies, the man now reaches to the *right* and grasps a new object, the duck rather than the frog. In this case, the babies see an *old movement* to get a *new object*. For the other half, the man reaches *left* and gets the frog. These babies see a *new movement* to get the *old object*.

The skits test how Susie and the other babies see the man's earlier reaches. Were those reaches merely a repetitive motion so that for no particular

---

* Spelke herself now has said, "All this time I've been giving infants objects to hold, or spinning them around in a room to see how they navigate, when what they really wanted to do was engage with other people! Why did it take me 30 years to start studying this?"

reason the man kept reaching right? Or, did the man reach there *because he wanted the frog*?

If babies see the original skit in terms of the man's wants and not simply his movements, then when he reaches for the frog (the *new movement* to reach the *old object*), that would be expected. The man gets the frog again. "Is that new for you?" "No."

But if the man used the old movement to reach a new object (the *old movement, new object* test skit) that should catch their attention. They expected the man to want the frog; instead, he reached for the duck. "Is that new for you?" "Yes!" That violated their expectation, even though the man used the same movement they'd already seen again and again.

Babies from four months on answer (figuratively), "Yes, that's unexpected," when the man reaches for the duck. They interpret the man as having desires: that man had reached for the frog because he wanted it. It's an infant's first step toward a theory of mind.

Or, is that interpretation too theory-of-mind driven? What if babies are really doing data mining, like Deep Blue or Temple Grandin? What if they're associating man and reach and frog and orange mat in some automatic way instead of seeing them as connected by the man's wants and goals.

As you may now expect, researchers worked out a skit to test that, as well. This is where my Baby Lab comes in. In our skits, a woman faces a transparent box full of small toys: fifteen ducks and five frogs.[6] Half the babies watch the woman take five ducks and no frogs from the box. This trial is repeated until the infant gets bored and almost stops watching. This is called the Majority skit. Adults who see a Majority skit say things like, "She always gets ducks because there are so many ducks," or "The ducks come more easily to hand."

Other infants watch a Minority skit. The woman again faces a box of ducks and frogs, but for this skit the box holds fifteen *frogs* and only five *ducks*. The woman takes all five ducks and no frogs from the box. This is repeated till the infant hardly watches. When adults explain a Minority skit, they say things like, "That lady really likes ducks," or "For some reason, she sure wants ducks."

Note that the babies and adults who watch either the Majority or the Minority skits see the same actions: a woman uses the same hand motion to take five ducks from a box of ducks and frogs (woman, grasp, five ducks, box). Yet adults seeing the Minority skit say the woman clearly wants ducks. They infer the woman's underlying mental state: a desire for ducks.

Impressively, that's what ten-month-old infants (the youngest infants we've tested so far) in our studies do too. How do we know? When the babies are bored with the Majority or Minority skit, we show them the test skit. For this skit, the woman is placed between two small transparent bowls, one of which holds frogs and the other ducks. The woman now reaches for either a frog or a duck.

When the woman reaches for a frog, the babies who have just seen the Minority skit look a lot. They thought she liked ducks, and now she reaches for a frog. It violates the babies' expectation. "That's something new."

Babies who have just seen the Majority skit where ducks fell easily to hand don't react much to *either* choice: "Same old, same old, once again the woman is taking an available toy."

Slightly older children, who can deliberately give and take things, can participate by handing a toy to the woman. At eighteen months, children choose to give the Minority skit woman a duck from the two small bowls; after all, that's what she liked when she chose for herself from the box. But, they give the Majority skit woman a frog, or a duck, or *both* because that woman didn't show an obvious liking for ducks, she just took what was at hand.

These skits make it clear that infants don't just mine data. At some level, they understand others' desires: This woman prefers ducks, or that man likes the frog. This is theory of mind in the making; it's how reading minds begins.

Further Questions

The idea that infants can understand others' desires at first seemed unlikely. But accumulating research has made it increasingly clear and accepted. Moreover, as research has continued, several at first surprising conclusions about babies have emerged, while several other questions remain under vigorous debate.

Primal Egocentrism?

For years, the prevailing wisdom was that babies begin life as deeply egocentric. Babies, thinking went, understand people only in terms of the baby's own acts and states; they can't register the acts and states of anyone else. Piaget said young infants are bound by their own sensory experiences: by *their* visual attention to things and by *their* motor actions, like sucking and grasping. They aren't able to separate their own experience (*I* see the bird and like it) from yours (*you* see the bird and like it).

That stands counter to the findings I've just shown. In the frog–duck studies, for example, when infants were asked to choose an animal for themselves, about half preferred frogs. If they were egocentric, then those infants should give the woman a frog. Seen egocentrically, she would want what they wanted, a frog. Yet, in the Minority skit, infants consistently gave the woman a duck. Cued by her previous choices, they figured out *her* desire. They saw she went out of her way to get the ducks, so they gave her a duck.

The broccoli–goldfish study I wrote about previously shows the same thing. Infants gave Betty the broccoli when she showed she liked broccoli best ("Yum!"), even when they, themselves, preferred the crackers.

Across numerous studies, research has shown that even at the age of ten months, babies understand that other people have desires of their own. At least some of the time, they understand: I like goldfish, but you like broccoli. Contrary to conventional wisdom, even young infants go beyond an egocentric understanding of others.

False Beliefs?

One area of particular dissension is whether infants understand false beliefs. If they did, it would be the nascent appearance of what will become a fully fledged theory of mind.

For years, researchers didn't even raise that question. Preschool studies were crystal clear: Children develop an understanding of false beliefs during the preschool years. And to support this, preschoolers also develop childhood lying, persuasion, and secret keeping, everyday uses of false belief. But then researchers began to ask: Might babies have an early understanding of false beliefs after all?

In 2005, Kristine Onishi and Renee Baillargeon launched a study that has served as the basis for research in this area.[7] Once again, their methods were based on what babies attend to when they're presented with skits that violate their expectations. And, indeed, Baillargeon gained her infant research expertise, like Amanda Woodward did, as a postdoctoral scholar in Elizabeth Spelke's laboratory.

In the first skit, a fifteen-month-old infant watched an adult place a toy red watermelon in a green box. Then, the baby, but *not* the adult, saw the toy moved to an adjacent yellow box.

In the test skit, the infants watched the adult reach into a box. Half the babies saw her reach into the green box, where the watermelon was originally. Half saw her reach into the yellow box, where the watermelon was moved without the adult's knowledge. Which test skit violated the infants' expectation?

A child who understood the adult thought the watermelon was still in its original location (a false belief) would expect the adult to reach into the green box. If, instead, the adult reached into the yellow box, the baby's false-belief expectation is violated. That infant should look at that event a lot. If the child doesn't understand false belief, he or she would expect the adult to look where the watermelon really is. That baby should look longer when the adult reaches into the green box.

In this study, infants gave the false-belief response. Fifteen-month-olds who saw the adult reach for the yellow box looked at that test event skit much longer than those who saw the adult reach for the green box.

But these results, unlike the research on infants' understanding of desires, to which Baillargeon also contributed, have not been duplicated consistently. Our Baby Lab could not obtain the same results. In a recent summary of replication studies, the German developmental scientist Hannes Rakoczy found that about half the attempts to find an understanding of false beliefs using violation-of-expectation measures fail. Overall, on the topic of infant understanding of false beliefs, we're faced with hard-to-decipher, fifty–fifty results.

Further, the successful results are said by their advocates like Bailargeon herself, to show an early form of implicit, innate understanding. According to this interpretation, the data show that babies understand false beliefs without learning. But the experiences of deaf infants of hearing parents refute that.

As I explained in Chapter 6, deaf children of hearing parents are slow to understand beliefs, false beliefs, and knowledge, probably because their early social and communication experiences slow their social learning. So, what about deaf infants? Do they show innate, unlearned false-belief understanding using Onishi and Baillargeon's methodology? If false-belief understanding is innate, it should appear on the same timetable for all infants, deaf or hearing, because it's built in to their development. If it's learned, the understanding would be delayed because deaf babies and children can't access social information due to hearing and language barriers.

In one of my favorite recent experiments, Marek Maristo and his colleagues in Sweden used a task like Onishi and Baillargeon's with deaf children as young as seventeen months.[8] These deaf infants did *not* show the false-belief response. Only older deaf children showed it, and their timetable for this was as delayed as their timetable for developing other theory-of-mind milestones. This suggests that innate false-belief understanding is highly unlikely.

Instead, theory-of-mind understandings, even those that typically appear in infancy, depend on both a child's experiences and the child's learning from those experiences. Consequently, some of those understandings appear very early in life, some come later.

Human Learning: The Real Baby Boom

We know much, but not everything, about how reading minds begins. This fuels continued debate about what is learned and what is innate in human social development. Elizabeth Spelke is convinced a huge piece of infant social understanding must be innate. She says babies show so much understanding about their social world so early they couldn't be learning it. According to Spelke, thousands of years of evolution have shaped humans to have some essential and distinctive features from birth: two legs, lots of vision, *and* an infant understanding that people have internal mental states.[9]

Some of this picture is obviously true. Humans have vision and two legs. They also pay keen attention to the social world around them, including some very early developing social insights like understanding that desires differ for different people. But this doesn't mean these are innate abilities. I believe that Spelke underplays the pivotal piece of our thinking that makes us uniquely human: We have an immense and innate ability to learn with incredible speed and enormous scope. This ability is our evolutionary endowment and advantage. Childhood learning is key to our character and nature. It defines us.

We are the species that adapts itself to the ecological niche where we find ourselves, not the niche where we began thousands of years ago. Other species survive by way of instincts adapted to their niche. Humans survive by being able to learn so we can adapt to almost any niche. We may achieve our adaptation through technology, clothing, hunting, agriculture, and the domestication of animals, but all of these are based on our ability to learn.

Our long and protected childhood is the special window for this pro-clivity to learn, and we can become lifelong learners as a holdover from this childhood ability. This leads us as adults to conduct science, to create mathe-matics, to produce poetry, and to invent life-sustaining technologies.

The point of this chapter is not just that babies know so much so early. They do. Infant understanding continues to be revealed and continues to astonish us. But believing infant understanding to be innate sells our hard-working babies short. The reason for infants' impressive understanding is their amazing capacity to learn quickly and from an early age.

Infants can assemble astonishingly sophisticated understandings in a matter of weeks. This is most evident in a baby's learning about the social world, a baby boom parents can watch with amazement. Babies learn by careful observation and by putting pieces together, like assembling blocks in a toy tower—a remarkable achievement for a speechless, uncoordinated being in a high chair. By age two, our children have built a foundation for all the social development that is to come.

The more researchers discover about social learning, the more many of us believe it grows even faster in infants and children than more observable skills like language. And, it is gained in similar huge bursts of accomplish-ment. That is how reading minds begins, and this social learning continues into adulthood. Block by block, we build new theories based on our earlier ones. The first glimmers of our ability to do this appear in infancy.

8

Superpowers, God, Omniscience, and Afterlife

When my grandson was almost five, he drew an illustrated chart of the superpowers of those around him. His mother could run across hot lava; his father could see long distances; his sister was very strong; his favorite stuffed animal could stay up late—past midnight.

As superpowers go, these are pretty tame, but they lead us into a world that young children are beginning to enter. It includes extraordinary abilities, abstract thinking, and concepts like God, superheroes, Hell, and omniscience.

This is not the terrain of preschoolers, in spite of their extraordinary learning, predispositions, and aptitudes. The abstract and profound world of the extraordinary opens for grade schoolers—like opening the door to *Narnia*—and then continues to be an area of discovery and learning into adulthood.

We see preschoolers start this journey with their love of dinosaurs and heavy construction equipment. The child is weak and powerless; T. Rex or a bulldozer is massive and effective. Trey could have watched road construction for hours.

Superheroes

Superheroes provide a next step as children's theory of mind moves them beyond thinking about the ordinary to wrestle with the extraordinary. Superman not only is big and strong, but also has superhuman abilities: He can fly, and he has x-ray vision. But Superman keeps one foot in the ordinary. He also has to eat, and he falls for Lois Lane. Superheroes, although super, are compared to tangible, known things that young children can understand. Superman is a man of steel, more powerful than a locomotive, faster than a speeding bullet.

Reading Minds. Henry M. Wellman with Karen Lind, Oxford University Press (2020) © Oxford University Press.
DOI: 10.1093/oso/9780190878672.001.0001

James Moor, of Parent dish UK (a now-defunct website for parents), told about his four-year-old asking for the millionth time to play superheroes with him:

> "OK," I said somewhat wearily.
> "Right," he said. "I'll be Batman and you can be Iron Man."
> "So what does Iron Man do then?" I said. It was clear he hadn't a clue.
> He thought for a moment and said: "Er, he does the ironing!"

What about ideas more extraordinary than special speed, extra strength, or fancy ironing? Deities, for example; most deities are almost completely abstract, unlike anything a child has experienced.

How Children Link to God

Interest in God often begins with partial understanding, and it also may first spring from children's interest in strength and power. When asked to draw God, younger children show him as more like a human with superpowers than a deity. A five-year-old drew God in uniform as "a superhero for the world." A nine-year-old drew him with "giant ears so he can hear everything we say."

As children mature, they go beyond this and begin to think about the extraordinary. British actress and author Monica Parker saw this when her seven-year-old son asked about God:[1]

> We told him that even though we can't see God, we believed God lives inside every living thing.
> The next morning, he came into our room and pronounced that he knew someone who HAD seen God—his doctor . . . when she cut people open to fix them, she would see God right inside.

From these beginnings[2] children reach for the concepts of God, omniscience, the afterlife, soul—concepts that theologians and many of the rest of us debate and struggle to understand throughout our lives. It is another area where children's more simplified beginnings can illuminate our more complicated destination.

This journey, I believe, tells an *anthropomorphism* story: Children begin by understanding the limited and fallible minds of ordinary people. From this base, they move toward an ever-expanding grasp of extraordinary minds.

There is an alternative story, however. It posits that young children have a special understanding of God because they have maintained a sense of their origins in God's presence. This view was first espoused by nineteenth-century Romantics, who believed children understood things about God an adult could not because their minds had not yet been contaminated by worldly experience. "Theirs' is the kingdom of heaven."

Justin Barrett pursued this idea. Barrett is a clever child development researcher and a devout religious believer who is a professor at Fuller Theological Seminary. He believed young children understood that God was infallible. To test this, he and his collaborators used a standard false-belief format.[3] They presented preschoolers with a cracker box, which the children expected would contain crackers. When it was opened, the box contained small rocks. The box was then reclosed, and the children were asked what Mom or God would think was in the box. Four- and five-year-olds often said Mom would not know the contents, the typical false-belief response. But, many said God would know. They attributed infallible knowledge to God.

Barrett argued that this supported a "preparedness" hypothesis rather than an anthropomorphic one. Children begin by being prepared to think of God as having higher understandings than humans. That are born believers.

Barrett's research inspired debate. One area of concern was that in his study, Barrett had grouped preschoolers into one-year age blocks. This grouping may have been too wide to show children's earliest beliefs. So, in follow-up studies, several of us, headed by Jon Lane—who is now a professor at Vanderbilt University—separated children into narrower age groups.[4]

Like Barrett, we asked children to judge how much different beings knew. We asked them about God; Heroman, who "can see right through things"; and ordinary humans, in particular Mom. Because we weren't sure if children knew that God had special mental abilities, we also introduced them to Mr. Smart. We told them Mr. Smart "knows everything about everything without looking," and we showed them his picture: an older man with an extra-large cranium and a wise, knowing look.

The youngest four-year-olds in our study were just beginning to attribute ignorance and false beliefs to ordinary humans. These children attributed the *same* limitations to God and to Mr. Smart as they did to humans. God, like Mom, would not know what was in the unopened box. Older four-year-olds and still older children mimicked the results from Barrett's study. They said God or Mr. Smart would know what was in the box, while Mom would not.

We conducted our research in the United States, where belief in an all-knowing being is prevalent. According to the Pew Research Center, over 90 percent of people living in the United States believe in a God,[5] so a basic childhood understanding of God should be common. We also recruited children who came from devout homes and attended religious preschools, children who we knew had received instruction about God from an early age.

Whether raised in secular or in religious homes, children clearly demonstrated anthropomorphism rather than preparedness. Religiously raised children hear earlier about God's extraordinary abilities, but they still must deal with these ideas using their limited childhood understanding. This is clear in a conversation a four-year-old brought from Sunday School:

> "The teacher said Jesus healed blind Bartimaeus. Later she said *God* healed Bartimaeus."
> I said, "I thought you said Jesus healed him?"
> And she said, "But Jesus is God."
> "Huh? How could God be his own son?"

Even when preschool children begin to credit God with extraordinary understanding—a special being knows more than Mom—that is a long way from understanding how far extraordinary mental capacities can exceed our limited human ones immensely. The steps children must take to reach that understanding are protracted and challenging because some of God's attributes are not easy to grasp, for either children or adults.[6]

Omniscience?

Omniscience is one of the most widely recognized attributes of an all-powerful God. Christian theologian James Packer explained:[7]

> Scripture declares that God's eyes run everywhere. He searches all hearts and observes everyone's ways. In other words, he knows everything about everything and everybody all the time. Also, he knows the future no less than the past and the present, and all his knowledge is always immediately and directly before his mind.

The Qur'an proclaims, "Allah knows whatsoever is in the heavens and whatsoever is on the earth. Verily, Allah is the All-Knower of everything." Buddhism holds that Gautama Buddha achieved an enlightened state in which he possessed extraordinary knowledge. Vishnu, a supreme Hindu god, is also described as omniscient.

Although adults easily and often say God knows everything, omniscience is a difficult, slippery concept, especially for children. One seven-year-old said:

> I learned Jesus knows everything, "even what the very hairs on your head are numbered." But there aren't enough numbers in the whole world to count Grandma's hairs.

In his book *The Spiritual Life of Children*, Robert Coles reported on a teenager who told him she talks with God but worries she's "asking for too much of his time."[8]

Understanding Superman requires no wrestling with omniscience. If Superman could read minds, he would know Lex Luthor's plans, foil them, and peace would reign in Metropolis: no good versus evil, no heart-pounding suspense, no drama.[9] So, when do we begin to understand omniscience, and what form does that take?

Jon Lane and I tried to discover what children, aged from three to eleven, as well as adults, understand about omniscience.[10] Because we weren't sure what children knew about God's omniscience, we again taught them about Mr. Smart, someone who knows "everything about everything." This time, we brought out a closed cardboard box that neither the child nor Mr. Smart had "ever seen before." Children were asked if they knew what was in the box.

"No," they answered. "It has a stapler inside," Mr. Smart said, and lo and behold, there was a stapler inside. "Mr. Smart knows *everything* about *everything*," we reiterated. And not just about boxes. "Do you know where this stapler was made? I don't, but maybe you do?" Children said no or just guessed. Quite a few said China. "Mr. Smart says, 'Canada.' Let's take a look." When turned over, the stapler had a sticker that read, "Made in Canada."

We gave several more demonstrations, always ending with, "Mr. Smart knows everything about everything! Without looking!" Until, when we asked them, "How much does Mr. Smart know?" the children answered,

"Everything!" So as much as we were able, in terms understandable to children, we had established that Mr. Smart was omniscient.

Then, we tried to discover how children applied this knowledge. First, we asked about God's, Mr. Smart's, or Mom's *breadth* of knowledge. Did any of these beings know, "What you're thinking right now?" "Where to find the world's largest tree?" "How hot the weather will be next summer?" Did any of them know about the past, present, and even the future? Did they know someone's private thoughts?

We then asked about these beings' *depth* of knowledge: their knowledge on a single area or topic, such as airplanes, cars, or planets. Did they know as much as an expert? "Who knows more about airplanes, a doctor or a pilot?" "Who knows more about airplanes, a pilot or Mr. Smart?"

By definition, an omniscient being's knowledge should surpass even an expert's knowledge because an omniscient mind knows *everything* about *everything*. This is different from our highly imperfect human understanding, even the understanding of experts. It is also different from the superpowers of superheroes. Omniscient minds are more than super.

Yet, we quickly found that preschoolers reported that an omniscient mind—God, or Mr. Smart—would be ignorant of many things. God or Mr. Smart would know more about medicine than Mom, but no more than a doctor. God or Mr. Smart would know a lot about airplanes, but no more (and maybe less) than an airplane pilot or an airplane mechanic.

As children grew older, they attributed more and more knowledge to God and Mr. Smart. But, even the eleven-year-olds in our study consistently attributed far less knowledge to an omniscient being than "everything about everything."

Does Religion Help?

Jon Lane and I wanted to explore this further: Would children with more religious training understand omniscience any better than those with less? For a second study, we tested children from devout homes who attended religious schools where they had received instruction about God and his powers.

Preschoolers from the devout, religiously schooled backgrounds said omniscient minds would be ignorant of many things just as their more secular peers had said. From ages three to eleven, children gradually attributed more knowledge to God and to Mr. Smart than to Mom. But even devoutly raised children, taught for years about God's extraordinary powers, said God and Mr. Smart (who they agreed knew everything about everything) would know more about airplanes than Mom, and more than a doctor, but *not* more than a pilot. Those who had more exposure to ideas about God attributed more knowledge to God somewhat earlier than those who had less. But even our oldest religiously reared children consistently attributed far less knowledge than "everything about everything" to an omniscient being.

Adults, Too

Adults find omniscience to be an elusive concept as well. In other studies, when U.S. adults were asked to make judgments about God's powers, many readily said God was omniscient and was unconstrained by perceptual limitations. But, they struggled when they tried to apply this practically.[11] They were told a brief story about many people praying to God at once. The same people who had talked clearly about God's omniscience said God would deal with a few prayers first and would deal with the others only later. In their everyday thinking, these adults defaulted to thinking God was constrained by more limited, human-like abilities—just like the teenaged girl who worried she was asking for too much of God's time.

The difficulty in conceptualizing total omniscience has been apparent to theologians for centuries. St. Augustine in the 1800s, and before him, St. Thomas Aquinas in the 1200s, noted that it is difficult to talk about a being who is completely "other." Without *any* sort of human-like limits for a backdrop, a completely unlimited mind cannot be grasped—by adults or by children.

The Living Dead

Almost 75 percent of U.S. adults, a number that includes Christians, Muslims, and many Jews, believe in life after death. An equal percentage believe that people who lead good lives will go to heaven, and according to a

2005 Harris Poll, about six in ten Americans believe in Hell, also an afterlife.*
Anthropological evidence suggests these beliefs go very far back. Some of the
earliest humans buried their dead with objects and food, presumably to sus-
tain them in an afterlife.

How do we explain that so many believe in an afterlife? When and how do
we come to these beliefs? This also requires going beyond early childhood
understanding.

By the early school years, most children understand that death terminates
bodily functions, happens to all living things, and is irreversible. But what,
if anything, do they understand about life after death? And when does their
understanding begin?

My friend Carl Johnson, a developmental psychologist at the University of
Pittsburgh, talked with his three-year-old daughter, Eve, after the mother of a
young friend of hers died:[12]

> I explained that when you die everything in your body stops working.
> I emphasized that the body is broken and it cannot be fixed. Finally, I indi-
> cated that the (dead, broken) body is buried.

The conversation was picked up a few months later when they were visiting
an art museum. Eve was shaken by a painting of Christ on the cross: "What
happened to him?"

> Carl read her *The Little Book of Jesus*, which told the Resurrection story.
> When I got to the part where Jesus died, was buried, but then came back
> to life, my daughter asked, "Is he dead or not?"
> The best I could come up with was that he was a special kind of person.
> She asked to hear the story again. Getting to the same part, where Jesus dies
> she again asked, "Is he dead or not?"
> I repeated the "special person" explanation. Unsatisfied, she concluded,
> "Kids can't understand this story."
> Several days later, Eve got out one of her favorite books, *The Body Book*.
> At the end of the book, a dead body is buried.

---

* Not all our prowess in thinking about and believing in extraordinary powers and states leads to
rosy conceptions, of course. Eternal suffering in Hell is a particularly devilish, undesirable form of
afterlife, for example. Children also encounter and wrestle with darker forms of extraordinariness.
A school-age child being instructed by nuns in a Catholic school told Robert Coles she'd asked a nun
what was the devil like, and the nun had said, "When he gets you, he'll never let you go."

She knew the book by heart, and proceeded to tell it to me, page by page. Like my instruction, it included the part where a dead body is buried. But what attracted my daughter was an additional element. After the body was dead and buried, there was a picture showing a flower growing on the gravesite. My daughter triumphantly explained, "The body is buried and a flower grew."

Problem solved: Life after death preschool style.

What happens as children step closer to adulthood?

Afterlife

Paul Harris and Marta Giménez asked preschoolers and kindergarteners in Spain about mind and also about "immortality." These children, educated in both religious and secular schools, were asked to judge the capabilities of God versus a friend on a number of topics. When asked about life, children from both secular and religious schools said God was less prone to die than the friend.

But, God's potential immortality is not the same as an afterlife for humans. So Harris and Giménez went on to ask children, ages seven and eleven years, about what happens after the death of a grandparent.[13] For this study, children heard one of two stories: one medical, the other religious.

In the medical story, a grandmotherly woman fell sick, asked to go to the hospital, went to the hospital, and had surgery. After some time in the operating room, the surgeon told the family she had died. With this story, only about 10 percent of the seven-year-olds thought *any* functions would continue after death. With the same story, about 60 percent of the eleven-year-olds thought some mental functions (like thinking of her grandchildren) would continue after death.

In the religious story, the grandmotherly woman fell ill and asked to see her priest. The priest came and sat with the woman in her room. After some time, the priest told the family she'd died. Given this religious story, about 50 percent of the younger children and 85 percent of the older children claimed that some of the grandmother's mental functions would continue after death.

These children showed definite developmental trends. The older children more often affirmed an afterlife. They were also more likely to say the continuing functions were mental not bodily ones. The grandmother would not eat or breathe, but she could miss her grandchildren and wish them well. Any of the younger children who said some functions survived death also said it was mental functions that survived.

Concepts like extraordinary knowledge and afterlife are built on foundational blocks. Children's earliest notions about extraordinary beings or capacities are based on human limitations and are mired in the everyday. Onto this base layer children can add more exotic information about mythic heroes like Achilles and Amazons or, in our society, their superhero counterparts Superman, Wonder Woman, and Iron Man. Later still, they can add understanding about still more abstract concepts: God, omniscience, and an afterlife.

Is Your Mind Invisible? Is Your Brain?

A surprising but important stepping stone toward understanding what is extraordinary comes when children begin to differentiate brain and mind.

Initially, children say brain and mind are the same. They are the place "where we do our thinking." Carl Johnson and I wanted to know when children started to separate the two.[14] We asked preschoolers to ninth graders, "Without a mind, can you think about a tree?" "Without a brain, can you think about a flower?" In addition to asking about mental acts like thinking and remembering, we asked them about sensations, like seeing and hearing; about voluntary behaviors, like tying your shoes and clapping your hands; and about involuntary behaviors, like breathing and sneezing.

Preschoolers, first graders, and even many third graders, said you needed your brain and mind only for purely "mental" acts: to think or to remember. Period. They indicated you don't need either one to see ("you just need your eyes"), to hear ("you just need your ears"), or to yawn ("you just need your mouth").

Fifth- and ninth-grade children knew the brain was necessary for all functions: for sneezing, for breathing, for yawning, as well as for seeing, reading, and thinking. These children said you can sneeze and yawn without a mind (your brain will take care of that), but you need a mind for thinking thoughts and feeling emotions. Further, the mind can sometimes be "on" and sometimes be "off," although the brain is always chugging along. These children understood mind and brain have different functions.

The Invisible Brain

As I've noted previously, preschoolers and first graders not only think thoughts and ideas are invisible, but Carl and I discovered that they also think the *brain* is invisible, because for them, brain = mind. One hundred percent of first graders who said the mind was intangible and invisible also said the brain was intangible and invisible. By third grade, and especially by fifth and ninth grades, children in our studies knew the physical brain was different from the nonphysical mind. By ninth grade, 90 percent thought brain and mind would be different. The brain, but not the mind, could be seen and touched by opening the head or by using a special x-ray machine.

Understanding that mind is separate from brain allows children to project an afterlife. The brain and the body can die, but because the mind is different, some of its functioning may continue after death. They can begin to understand a God that has no body but has immense mentality. They can even contemplate a soul.

The Soul Has It

What aspect of a person is most likely to transcend death? Adults are most likely to say a person's spirit. We consider this more likely than that the person's mind (which we judge as somewhat likely) or body (which we judge as unlikely) would continue. This is also true in religious traditions, where the aspect of a person most likely to transcend death is the spirit or soul.

Rebekah Richert and Paul Harris asked grade schoolers what functions would continue beyond death: bodily functions (like breathing), sensory functions (like sight), mental functions (like memory), or spiritual functions (soul).[15] These children said the soul was more likely to continue than thoughts or memories and vastly more likely to continue than breathing, seeing, or hearing.

In a related experiment, five- to twelve-year-olds were shown a scenario of an infant baptism and asked what difference the baptism would make. Even the youngest children said baptism would result in an invisible/intangible change. At all age groups, children said baptism most changed the soul, somewhat changed the mind, and had almost no effect on the brain.

Mind, brain, body, soul, limits, powers—children's deepening understandings of these concepts allow their deepening exploration of religion, as well as their understanding of and attraction to heroes, super-heroes, enchanted princesses, and other beings where mind and body exotically relate: zombies, vampires, and brain transplants (Sidebar 8.1).

Sidebar 8.1 Mind, Body, and Identity

Imagine a brain transplant: Someone has your body and your appearance as well as your stomach, eyeballs, hair, and ears but has someone else's brain and thoughts. For an adult, that wouldn't be you. But young children don't share this idea. It is only when children can differentiate mind and brain that they can understand personal identity.

Carl Johnson[16] showed children in kindergarten through fourth grade a drawing of a pig, Garby, in a pigpen. Garby's likes were compared to the child's: Garby loved to sleep in slop (instead of a bed); he had pig friends (rather than child friends); he had memories of being a pig (vs. memories of being a boy). Children were then asked to pretend that something happens: "We'll pretend to take your brain out of your head and put it inside Garby's head."

"What about now? With your brain, would this pig like to sleep in slop, or would he want to sleep in a bed?" "With your brain, would this pig have memories of being a pig or memories of being a boy?" "Suppose we call this pig to come home, would he come when we said 'here Garby,' or would he come when we said 'here [child's name]'?"

Until second grade (about age seven or eight), the children didn't see the consequences of a brain transplant on a person's being, thinking, or identity. Almost 90 percent of first graders said that with the child's brain, the pig would like sleeping in slop and would have pig memories. By fourth grade, more than 90 percent of the children said with their brain, Garby would want to sleep in a bed. Equally, older children said the pig would not have pig memories. Instead, "He'd have *my* memories!"

Although younger children say the brain is needed to think and remember, they don't see the brain as holding personalized memories, thoughts, preferences, and identity. They don't recognize that giving you a different brain would mean "you" are a different you. Not until age seven to eight years do U.S. children typically grasp that the brain, because it houses the mind with all its thoughts, is essential to a person's being and identity.

Transcending the Ordinary

Everyday childhood thinking about the ordinary puts us on a path that eventually leads us to God, mind, spirit, and the afterlife. It's a path that requires a long journey of overlapping phases.

Babies form understandings that help them make sense of a practical world where people have preferences and act intentionally on tangible objects. During preschool, their understanding is organized into a theory of mind that says people act to get what they *think* they *want*. This theory becomes the foundation for grade schoolers' ideas about superpowers and extraordinary beings, God, Wonder Woman, and life after death. It is also the foundation for building concepts like omniscience, immortality, omnipotence, and the soul.

This higher level thinking can then allow still deeper, more complex philosophical and theological questions: How are mind and body, soul and matter, ideas and reality, belief and faith related? Is mind just a product of matter, or is matter a reflection of mind? Is our ultimate reality material or spiritual?

Although thinking and reasoning at this level embrace increasingly extraordinary ideas, those ideas also are anchored in our earlier, ordinary, childhood thinking about ordinary minds, brains, people, and bodies.

9

Possible Worlds, Possible Minds

A man walks by you wearing white face paint, an elaborate animal headdress, and a dried-leaf skirt. Depending on your culture, you may, rightly, label him a shaman, a devil, a lunatic, or an early trick-or-treater.

Our adult social worlds and social thoughts differ, sometimes starkly, from one culture to another. What is normal in one may be considered bizarre in another; what is fascinating and central in one group's thinking can be uninteresting and peripheral to another group's. Anthropologists talk about this as a culture's folk psychology: the framework and beliefs that form the group's understanding of people and their actions. That these folk psychologies differ is an anthropological truism, one readily endorsed by anyone who has lived for a time in another country.

But this truth becomes strange when we contrast our immense adult differences with where those understandings began in childhood. As I've shown in previous chapters, at one point in their lives, children worldwide hold similar theories about how people work. They do so in Africa, China, the United States, or any of dozens of other cultures studied worldwide.

How can widely divergent adult beliefs about people spring from the same childhood theories? And if they do, can they really be so widely divergent?

When People Don't Care

Since the late 1970s, Cornell University ethnopsychologist Jane Fajans has studied the Baining, a traditional group living in the interior of New Guinea.[1] She claims the Baining's traditional view of people cannot be considered very psychological at all:

The most challenging and interesting thing about the Baining, is that they appear not to have a folk psychology. If folk psychology includes a concern

Reading Minds. Henry M. Wellman with Karen Lind, Oxford University Press (2020) © Oxford University Press.
DOI: 10.1093/oso/9780190878672.001.0001

with affect and emotions, concepts of person and self, theories of deviance, interpretations of behavior, and ideas about cognition and personality, the Baining manifest very little interest in these areas.

Ethnopsychology is a specialty within anthropology that looks primarily at the ideas and practices of traditional peoples. It emphasizes how a people understand the way humans act and think, how they psychologize their social worlds or perhaps fail to do so.

According to Fajans, the Baining consider people, themselves and others, in terms of their behavior and social roles rather than considering their internal psychological states. Desires, intentions, thoughts, knowledge, and emotions play little part in their interactions.

Generally, Baining adults chew betel nut daily. They say betel kills worms, "beautifies the mouth," and provides general purification. Betel nut has a mild stimulating effect (confirmed in laboratory tests), so it also is said to increase alertness and a sense of well-being. It is not unlike drinking coffee for many in our Starbucks-obsessed world.

Fajans interviewed a woman, Pinam, who did not chew betel nuts or drink the sap of a tree that is used as an alternative when betel nuts are scarce. When Fajans asked her why she didn't use betel nuts, the woman offered a story from her past.

> When I was young, I went with some women to the bush. We went to a certain tree [whose sap had the betel nut substitute]. We took this sap like betel nut and chewed it with lime. We chewed and chewed and chewed. Then I vomited and vomited and vomited. I said I would never chew betel again. I left behind me a large packet of the sap, but the other women went back and fought over it and took it.

In Western society, this kind of "why" question usually elicits a theory-of-mind explanation, but Pinam didn't do that. We don't hear, "I felt terrible," "I wish I'd never chewed it," "I hate betel." Instead, she described only her actions. She chewed the sap, she vomited, and she said she would never chew it again.

When Fajans asked Pinam why she didn't smoke tobacco (also very unusual in Baining society), Pinam told another story that again had no reference to her mental states. Fajans then said:

Pinam's stories were told in a house occupied by three generations of Pinam's descendants. All of them knew well that she neither smoked nor chewed betel nut, and said so when I would offer her betel nut or tobacco. However, no one in the house had ever heard these stories before. People laughed and enjoyed the stories, which had never arisen spontaneously. This was so even though everyone knew the tree she mentioned, and had seen the cuts in the bark where the sap had been drained.

The members of Pinam's family knew Pinam did not chew betel or smoke tobacco, but had never asked "Why?" They were not interested in a question Westerners ask constantly from age two on.

The distant Baining seem to have a vastly different theory of mind compared our own, but surprisingly close to home are theories of mind that differ almost as widely.

When God Talks Back

When God Talks Back is the title of a book by Stanford anthropologist Tanya Lurhmann.[2] She wrote about her observations and study within an evangelical church, the Church of the Vineyard, which has branches in many cities with hubs in Chicago and near San Francisco. In this church, the preacher and the congregation believe they can recognize when God, in the form of Jesus, is present and open to conversation with them.

In my Methodist upbringing, and in the beliefs of my Methodist preacher grandfather, God was not someone who talked to you regularly and conversationally. But at the Church of the Vineyard, God talks to congregants often and about specific things. This might include not only big decisions like where to go to college, but also mundane ones like what to wear to church that day. Because conversations are private, within one's mind, "Someone who worships at Vineyard must develop the ability to recognize thoughts in their own mind that are not in fact their thoughts, but God's." This takes practice and guidance because in our everyday theory of mind, mind and world are separate. The Church of the Vineyard

demands that one set out to develop a new theory of mind. It is not radically different from the basic theory of mind that toddlers acquire. But this new Christian theory of mind—we could call it a "participatory" theory of mind—asks congregants to experience the mind-world barrier as porous.

This porousness is used in one area only: for private conversation with God.

To revise one's theory of mind in this way, even though it is "not radically different," requires sustained work for newcomers to Vineyard. To do the needed work, they are given support from preachers and support and instruction within the church's prayer groups and "prayer teams."

Mind Overcomes Reality

Buddhist understandings and teachings about mind provide another counterpoint to Western theories of mind. In Western theory of mind, adults say that thinking occurs in a stream of consciousness: "chain-reaction-like flashings of whole sequences of thoughts, each cueing its successor." Our everyday understanding is that mental states of perception, knowing, and recognizing connect the inner self to the outer "real" world.

Mahayana Buddhism ("the Great Vehicle") is one of the two great streams among the many Buddhist teachings and traditions.[3] It originated in India a bit before the time of Christ, then spread to Tibet, China, Indochina, Japan, Korea, and beyond.

According to Mahayana Buddhist thought, our everyday understanding and experience of mind is deceptive and flawed. Stream of consciousness is a symptom of a "monkey mind": unsettled and unsettling, confused and capricious. Further, our belief that the mind connects the self to the real world mires us in cravings—external attractions and repulsions, wants and aversions. Our beliefs about mind, self, and reality perpetuate a malicious interconnection: Monkey mind connects the self to external attractions and repulsions that bounce us around in ignorance and suffering.

Buddha's great enlightenment was his understanding that mind and reality are fundamentally different from our deceptive, everyday impression. Through practices and guidance, like mindfulness training, Buddhists can instead discover two truths. First, we can control the monkey mind and immerse ourselves in a universal, enduring consciousness, attentive to the present moment, rather than a flitting stream of consciousness. Second, reality consists of blissful serenity rather than a kaleidoscope of thoughts, attractions and repulsions. Buddhist monks have engaged in and perfected these practices and doctrines over centuries. Waves of cultural importation, most recently the Dalai Lama's appearances, have brought these ideas to the West.

The Baining, the renewalist evangelicals, and Buddhists endorse folk psychologies that are quite different from one another and different from the theory of mind I have described previously.[4] Yet, even in the face of these dramatic differences, I am convinced everyday theory of mind, of the sort I've talked about, is universal.

People Everywhere Are Different, People Everywhere Are Just the Same

In logic, a contradiction is a sign of defeat, but in the evolution of real knowledge it marks progress toward a victory.
—Alfred North Whitehead[5]

How can both these contradictory claims be true: Theory of mind is universal, but folk psychologies differ profoundly? The answer rests in development.

Teaching and Time

One crucial aspect of this development is change based on teaching and guidance. As Lurhmann explained, these can help adults rewrite their prior understanding of mind. Church of the Vineyard members learn to shift their everyday understanding of the boundary between mind and world to become porous to God's presence.

More change, and more radical change, can be accomplished if teaching and guidance are begun in childhood and are woven into a child's unfolding life. We know that socialization in children's homes, families, and cultural communities influences theory of mind. Children in China, recall, rise on the Theory-of-Mind Scale via a different sequence than children in the United States. Omniscience and superheroes are apprehended step by step.

Not only do individuals develop theory of mind over their lives, but also communities and cultural groups revise and perfect their understandings over generations. Lurhmann provided one contemporary example:

It's a big promise for Vineyard Church to claim that any Christian will be able to feel unconditionally loved by God. And the promise of unconditional love is not an inevitable interpretation of the Christian God. For much of the history of Christianity, Christians have feared God. The great scenes that stretched above the church doors of medieval Europe showed Christ sitting in judgment.

My Methodist grandfather preached about God's love, often using Paul as his text. In Corinthians, Paul says, "Love is patient, love is kind. . . . It is not easily angered, it keeps no records." At the same time, he preached about the distance between God and man. God is awesome, impressive, and daunting. He inspires not only admiration, but also apprehension and fear. My grandfather preached on God's forgiveness, but he preached on God's judgment and wrath as well.

Luhrmann continued:

The God of the renewalist evangelical church is not this cruel judge. The Vineyard took the basic Christian narrative about the distance between a limited human and a boundless almighty God and shifted the plotline from our inadequacy to God's extraordinary capacity. Gone is the fear of snapping the connection. Gone is the fear of the abyss. The story becomes God's infinite and personal love that can be had now today, as long as you accept that God is loving; that God is present; and above all, that God loves *you*, just as you are, with all your pounds and pimples.

Contemporary renewalist evangelical churches, like the Vineyard, have been revising and perfecting their understandings since the 1960s. Decades went into developing their communities' beliefs and practices. To form a Christian understanding that is both recognizably Christian but distinctively "renewed" took time and a succession of cohorts. Buddhism has had centuries of development, with one byproduct being the variety of forms of Buddhism practiced worldwide. Change over time is a critical element in explaining how folk psychologies can be universal and at the same time widely different across peoples and communities.

Also critical is grasping that theory of mind, like any theory, exists at both basic and at more specific levels. The basic think–want structure operates as a "framework theory of mind." The details added to it give us specific theories of mind. The think–want framework allows us to understand Eva

Longoria's actions discussed in Chapter 2 generally: She acts to get what she wants. Beyond that, Longoria fills in this framework with specific details. She created her foundation because, "I'm Latina, and this community needs help." She wanted to do something and "wanted to focus on education," so her foundation helps "Latina women improve their lives through education." She's happy and proud of the successes of her foundation. We understand these pieces because we understand the basic think–want framework as well as the need for details to fill it.

The framework is like a skeleton; the specifics are like the meat on the bones. Each needs the other, and *both* can develop and change over time, like a child's bones and muscles change as they grow.

Rubber-Band Development

So, how can theory of mind be not only universal but also profoundly different? The short answer is that universal processes and beginnings can allow and propel the development of vastly different belief systems. The secret is how this all plays out.

What humans, especially human children, share worldwide is a framework theory of mind. By age two or three, children in the United States, the United Kingdom, India, Peru, Micronesia, China, Japan, and Iran expect people to have thoughts, wants, perceptions, and feelings. These assumptions develop from infant proclivities such as their preference for faces, for social interaction, and for seeing another's point of view.

The meat children put on those bones is more specific to their own culture: What do *my* people think? For instance, are cows think–want agents like people? (They are in India.) Should I prefer individualized beliefs over consensual knowledge? (Yes, I should in the United States; no, I shouldn't in China.) What sort of emotions are good, bad, and "ideal" for people to cultivate and show? (Active exuberance and excitement are ideal in Western, individualistic societies, but calm, peaceful harmony is preferred in many Eastern, collectivist societies.)[6] Is God awesome or infinitely loving?

The skeleton frames the learning of details. The details are specific to a community, and the whole system is dynamic. In human anatomy, the bones shape the body's muscle mass while the muscles shape the skeleton. Constant swimming helps shape the swimmer's body: Broader shoulders result from muscles working on the shoulder bones and rib cage.

In theory-of-mind framework development, the skeleton develops *and* it frames further development, including the specifics we learn. The framework both enables and constrains the specifics we learn because we have developmental learning limits. This is a *rubber-band* model of developmental learning.[*] We can't learn anything and everything even though our childhood allows many years for this learning to take place. Children's minds can stretch only so far.

This is where history—development over years and across generations or cohorts—can help. Over centuries, groups and societies can move from travel by foot, to horseback, to trains, to automobiles, to airplanes, to jets, to space shuttles. They can go from an Old Testament God, to a New Testament God, to an evangelical personal-friend God. They can end up with artifacts like an abacus and computer that are far removed from the finger counting where they began. And their political beliefs can move from the divine right of kings, to *liberté, égalité, fraternité,* and on to comrade.

Cultural changes that unfold over history can be extensive and exotic, but they also have their rubber-band limits. Any culture can stretch, expand, and twist to create various novel ideas about mind by starting from the basics. Or, it can diminish mind by focusing on behaviors and spoken words, as seems to be true with the Baining. The result can be very different folk psychologies among different folk. But, folk psychologies cannot stretch infinitely. Their tenets must be something that children of the community can learn. If an idea pulls the rubber band too far, it breaks. When children can't learn some novel ("unnatural") idea, the chain of transmission fails.[†]

Contradictions and Progress

It may appear to be a contradiction that theory of mind is universal while folk psychologies are radically different in one place versus another. But, embracing both things as true marks progress toward real knowledge, as Alfred North Whitehead asserted.

---

[*] I first heard and contributed to this metaphor in a conversation with Tanya Luhrmann in her office at Stanford. To my mind, it nicely captures how our understandings can be elastic, within limits, and at the same time how basic understandings can bind together many others.

[†] It should actually be impossible to find clear, understandable examples of totally unnatural folk psychologies. The historical record shows us ideas that have persevered across time and generations. It erases exotic ideas that someone may have had but no one else could learn.

Universal social cognition exists, as we see in childhood theory of mind. Of course, no single cultural group's children show us *the* universal, culture-free theory of mind because children begin cultural learning at birth. Yet, taken together, children worldwide illuminate the universal framework because in them we can see learning and development in their earliest stages.

As you might now expect, adults' conceptions of people are less similar worldwide than children's. Cultures have centuries in which to develop unique understandings of persons, selves, and societies. A society then has years to stretch a child's universal framework and teach its unique beliefs and worldviews. The resulting adult folk psychologies can be and are quite different from one another worldwide. At the same time, all of them are grounded in the same initial framework of young children.

10

Chimps, Dogs, and Us

The Evolution of Reading Minds

You may have seen documentaries of Jane Goodall sitting on the ground in the wilds of an African jungle, watching chimpanzees. A well-known one is the BBC production *Jane Goodall's Wild Chimpanzees*. When it was made, Goodall had been studying the same chimpanzees in Gombe National Park, Tanzania, for more than forty years. By 2018, she had been at it more than fifty-five years, the longest continual study of chimpanzee behavior ever.[1]

Breaking with established anthropological tradition, Goodall gave her chimps names not numbers—David Greybeard, Flo, and her children Fifi, Figan, and Frodo—and she described their individual personalities. Frodo was a "bully" and a thug. "Surprisingly, brutal as he may be, Frodo has a soft and gentle side as well," she has said. Gigi was a childless adult female who "delighted in being 'aunt'" to many young chimps. David Greybeard was the first chimp to warm to Goodall. He befriended her and fostered social relations that led to her being accepted as a member of the troop.

Goodall asserted, "It isn't only human beings who have personality, who are capable of rational thought, and emotions like joy and sorrow." Her interpretations seem most believable when you see her chimps go beyond eating and grooming. A mother carries, plays with, and tickles her infant; a male kisses another infant; or a female protects someone else's child. "I've seen so much here at Gombe. Political intrigue, cruelty, war, but also love, compassion and even humor." Goodall says her chimpanzees engage in these and other "human" behaviors.

How Human Are They?

Chimpanzees are our closest animal kin; we share more than 95 percent of the same DNA. Scientists—primatologists—study them for clues about what our early primate forebears must have been like and to better understand

Reading Minds. Henry M. Wellman with Karen Lind, Oxford University Press (2020) © Oxford University Press.
DOI: 10.1093/oso/9780190878672.001.0001

the gap that evolution overcame in producing human primates from prior nonhuman ones. Animal studies are a crucial way to discover what makes us uniquely human. What differentiates us from the rest of the animal kingdom? Is it tool use and bipedalism? Or, does it draw from a different source?

In the late 1890s, European explorers of Africa first began to describe primates: chimpanzees and gorillas. Their descriptions were of fearsome beasts with savage, unfathomable ways. The gap from them to us at that point seemed enormous in spite of their vaguely human-like looks. But, Goodall's findings showed ways in which our similarities go beyond genes to include similarities in intelligence, emotions, and social relations, along with politics and cultural traditions.

Goodall's depiction of chimpanzees has supported a rich vision of primate social cognition: a view of chimpanzees as our cousins and of their social cognition as close to ours. An early wave of chimp language-learning studies endorsed this view.[2] In the 1970s, Washoe, a female chimpanzee, was filmed using almost 300 signs from American Sign Language (ASL) to talk fluently with Beatrix and Allen Gardner, her owners, about things, people, and herself. Washoe was treated as a member of the Gardner family.*

But this is only one side of a seesawing, unfolding scientific debate. In addition to these rich, human-centric views of primates, there are also the lean.

Rich or Lean?

The Lean

In the 1980s and 1990s, laboratory testing began to show a much less generous picture of chimpanzee's social understandings. For one thing, chimp language was shown to be severely limited and not nearly as human-like as once thought. More lean evidence was provided by Daniel Povinelli, from his primate† laboratory in Louisiana, and Michael Tomasello, from his primate laboratory in Germany, along with their colleagues. Their influential studies suggested that chimps understand almost nothing about the psychological causes of behavior—not the perceptions, intentions, or beliefs that underlie

---

* When she became adolescent and attained her adult size, teeth, and strength, she was transferred out of any human family to a research station.
    † From here on, I mostly refer to primates as separate from humans. That's a shorthand for saying nonhuman primates versus humans because, of course, humans are also primates.

human actions. Their research on chimps' understanding of what others see was the most telling.

I saw this firsthand when I visited Danny Povinelli in his primate cognition lab in New Iberia, Louisiana, the heart of Cajun country. On flat acreage, barely above sea level, thousands of monkeys and hundreds of chimpanzees were housed on an old Air Force base. Most of the animals were available for biomedical research, but Povinelli's laboratory was dedicated to behavioral research on chimps—using their behavior as a window into their minds.

Povinelli's studies were based on chimpanzees' natural begging:[3] They use an outstretched hand to try to get food from other chimps. In his experiments, the apes were trained to beg from a trainer seated behind a clear Plexiglas wall in a testing room. The wall had several holes, but the chimps were supposed to gesture through the hole directly in front of the trainer. When they did, the trainer praised them and gave them a small food reward. All the apes quickly learned to beg from the trainer through the correct hole.

Once the chimps learned this, the study was launched. What would the apes do when they faced two trainers, one who could see them and one who could not? Obviously, a human would go to the trainer who could see them, but would the chimps?

Povinelli and his staff tried several alternative scenarios. Among those I saw was the *front–back* version. One trainer, dressed in soft-green surgical scrubs, sat facing the chimp, while another, dressed similarly, faced away. In *buckets*, one trainer's head was covered with a bucket while the other held an identical bucket beside her head. In *hands*, one trainer held her hands over her eyes; the other held her hands over her ears. Each pair included one person that a human immediately would know couldn't see them alongside another we would know could.

What happened? For the front–back scenario, apes gestured to the person facing them at a rate greater than chance. But that was the only version where the apes performed above chance in all the scenarios Povinelli presented. For every other scenario, the chimps were as likely to beg from a researcher whose head was in a bucket or whose hands completely covered her eyes as from one who looked directly at them. In contrast, two- and three-year-old human children go almost unerringly to the researcher who can see them.

What does this mean? Why are the chimps begging from testers who can't see them when they clearly want the food? Povinelli concluded that although apes are clever learners in many ways—able to learn to go to one bush or tree rather than another for tasty fruit, able to quickly learn to beg through the

Plexiglass hole when there was just one trainer sitting there—they are unable to use another's mental state, in this case perception, to solve a problem.

This was a very lean picture.

To test his hypothesis further, Povinelli and his staff returned to the front–back comparison, the only scenario that suggested the chimps might be clued to the trainers' perception. Again, they presented the apes with two trainers. This time, both of their bodies faced away, but one had her head twisted forward—the *head-over-shoulder* trainer. The chimps begged at a rate no better than chance from these two, although to humans the head-over-shoulder trainer could obviously see them, while the one whose head faced away could not. The apes seemed to have understood that body position could be a cue to being fed, but they didn't recognize that seeing was the critical factor.

The researchers also tested to see if the chimps could learn to use a trainer's perception. The apes were given numerous trials with different scenarios (*head over shoulder, buckets, hands, blindfold*). On each one, they got food only if they begged from the trainer who could see them, somewhat like rats reinforced with food in a Skinner box. For some of these scenarios, such as buckets, the chimps did eventually learn which was the correct trainer, but it was laborious, slow learning that took them hundreds of trials. Human children given similar trials are successful on their first attempt.

In the other scenarios, the chimps never performed above chance. In one of these, the chimps saw one trainer with a black blindfold tied over her eyes and another with the same black cloth tied over her mouth—an *eyes-mouth* contrast. Chimps begged equally to both trainers even after many, many trials where they were rewarded only if they begged to the "mouth" trainer. Further studies showed that as long as equal amounts of the trainer's face were covered, apes chose randomly. It didn't matter to them that one person could see them.

Throughout the 1990s, both Povinelli and, in independent research, Michael Tomasello[4] confirmed that chimpanzees are able learners for several key things: Chimps learned quickly if the trials involved the physical and social structures of their own world. They could quickly learn which others were dominant for food and sex. They could learn who to choose for allies. Females migrate to other groups at sexual maturity, so males learn brothers are better long-term allies than sisters. They learn to protect themselves. Males from other groups can kill neighboring chimps, so groups learn to post sentries at their territory borders. But this learning has, the researchers asserted, a major limitation compared to our own. Chimps can learn little or nothing about what drives an individual's actions, attention, or emotional expressions. This seemed to be a profound difference between humans and other primates.

Getting Richer

Fast-forward ten years, and I'm visiting Mike Tomasello at his primate cognition lab at the Leipzig Zoo in Germany. Why? Because since the 1990s, research had turned toward a richer view. Chimps are more like us than we'd thought. One experiment in particular compelled a sea change. It emerged from the continued efforts of Tomasello and his colleagues in Leipzig.[5]

On the surface, Tomasello's setup and experimental approach was much like Povinelli's. Animal trainers, mostly woman in soft-colored surgical scrubs, moved chimpanzees in and out of caged research rooms where they faced several carefully crafted scenarios. But in these experiments, chimps interacted competitively and with other chimps instead of with humans. That produced different results.

Chimpanzees are very hierarchical; there is a clear pecking order for males and females, males and males, and females and females. In Tomasello's study, two chimpanzees, one dominant and one subordinate, were placed behind doors across a room from each other. Food was placed in the central room, and the doors could be cracked so the chimps could peer into that room but could not enter to get the food. Small rectangular panels could be placed so different chimps could or could not see the food.

In nature, when a dominant and a subordinate chimp compete for food, the subordinate knows he will lose, so he lets the dominant go first. But in this setup, the competition could be controlled. In some trials, both saw the food; in others, the subordinate saw food when the dominant did not.

Tomasello wondered if a subordinate chimp could understand enough about the dominant chimp's perceptions to go after food the dominant couldn't see. And, in fact, when the subordinate chimps saw two pieces of food and knew the dominant chimp saw only one, the subordinate regularly went for the food the dominant couldn't see.

Does that mean, after all, chimpanzees can adjust their behavior based on what another sees? Can they recognize another chimp's perceptions and attention?

Seeing the chimps' behavior firsthand was convincing, and research has supported this richer view. In the Leipzig experiments, subordinates were able to determine the dominant's ability to see, or not see, from the first trial and in a variety of different situations. For example, Tomasello and his team wondered if having a dominant see food that was then hidden, tainted the food for subordinates, marking it as "for dominants only." If so, the chimps were operating from something like a food taboo rather than from an understanding of the dominant's ability to see. But in a variation of the task, one dominant saw the food hidden but was then swapped for a different dominant chimp who had never seen the food. In that case, the subordinate chimp quickly took the food. They were tracking the dominants' vision not steering away from a food taboo.

These studies confirmed that chimpanzees understand the link between seeing and knowing. If the dominant chimp saw, he would know.

Chimp Limitations

In a competitive situation, chimpanzees can understand what another ape (or a human, it also turns out) might see or know. They also understand some intentional actions, like whether the experimenter intends to give them a grape (Sidebar 10.1). But chimps can't understand another's beliefs or false beliefs, even in a competitive situation. Moreover, they virtually never teach; they don't even try. Teaching is an activity that requires theory-of-mind understanding. Even two-year-old humans try to teach others and are often successful. Neither young chimps nor adult chimps teach. Chimp moms don't even deliberately teach their children crucial food-getting skills.

Chimpanzee understanding falls far short of human children's. And children's actions seem to spring from a different, human, impetus altogether.

Sidebar 10.1 Other Primate Understandings

Tomasello and his colleagues have provided other information about how chimpanzees understand self and others. For example, note that in the food competition studies, the chimpanzees were tracking someone else nonegocentrically. They demonstrated an understanding of "I see it, you don't" or "I saw it hidden, and you didn't." When humans do this, from around the time of their first birthday on, scientists say they are employing visual or cognitive perspective taking. Our primate cousins do this as well.

The food competition results opened additional questions as well: How well do primates understand mental states like intentions? Could a richer view hold there as well?

Results from experiments involving *unwilling* versus *unable* interactors show that primates understand some revealing and subtle distinctions.[12]

In the primate version of an *unwilling–unable* experiment, Josep Call, along with Tomasello, engaged chimpanzees at the Leipzig Zoo in a procedure where a human trainer offered the chimp some food through the chimp's cage bars. For some chimps, the trainer tried to offer them a grape but was unable to give it to them. The tester repeatedly, clumsily, dropped a grape that rolled back to her rather than to the chimp. For other chimps, the tester offered, but then withdrew, a grape. From a human point of view, it seemed she was unwilling to part with the grape. Chimpanzees begged more and left the testing room earlier when an experimenter was unwilling to give them food than when she was unable to do so. In the unable situation, they were more patient and tolerant. This was true even though the trainer's behaviors (holding something out but not passing it on) and outcomes (the chimps did not get a grape) were remarkably similar.

Although the experimenter's actions appear to be similar, both chimpanzees (and in other research) human infants recognize a difference in the testers' underlying intentions, and they react accordingly.

Human Versus Chimp: Sharing, Helping, and Acquiring

Sharing and Cooperation

Chimps rarely share food. In both experimental trials and in the wild, chimps don't point out food to other chimps or readily give food to begging chimps.

Mothers will occasionally share food with their own children, but this is unusual, while human mothers and children share all sorts of things.

Some cooperation between chimps can be engineered in laboratory situations. Two chimps will work in tandem, pulling ropes attached to different ends of a tray, if that is the only way to get a food treat resting on the tray. But, once they have the food, unless the food is predivided, cooperation unravels, and the dominant chimp takes it all. This is very different from humans. Even very young children cooperate on tasks, and if the spoils are not predivided, they attempt to divide them equally.[6]

Helpful Disclosures

Sustained cooperation requires trust in a helpful partner. ("You'll share food with me.") It also often requires communication. ("You do this; I'll do that.") Povinelli's studies were based on these requirements. It proved to be the helpful–cooperative component that made the tasks difficult for chimps.

Further research showed that the key difference between Povinelli's studies and Tomasello's more recent ones was not that the interactor was a human rather than a chimp. Instead, it was having to read minds in a helpful–cooperative situation. In competitive experiments like those later pioneered by Tomasello, nonhuman primates show an understanding of the perceptions and knowledge of humans as well as of primates.

Humans, even very young children, use gestures, pointing, and later words to inform others. Eighteen-month-old Sammie will point to his favorite, but out-of-reach, stuffed animal so Mom gets it for him: imperative communication. Sammie will also point to a passing truck just so his Mom will notice it: declarative communication.

A large part of human communication is declarative. Studies have shown that by the age of two years, 80 percent or more of children's points are declarative: sharing an interesting event or sight with someone else. In contrast, virtually all ape communications are imperative and self-serving. When chimpanzees gesture to humans, about 95 percent of the time they are trying to get the human to give them something. They're begging.

If you watched the Jane Goodall documentaries, you might think an exception to this is when chimpanzees give calls that lead to food sharing. Chimp X finds a bunch of wild mangos, calls excitedly, and the other chimps rush in to eat. However, contemporary research suggests these calls are mainly self-serving. The chimp will call even when the entire group is near the mango tree and doesn't need further information. Instead, researchers say, chimpanzees call to have company while eating, as protection against predators, or simply from excitement. The function of the calls is not to inform or to share.

Helpful Acts

In contrast, Felix Warneken, a colleague of mine at Michigan, has shown how often and how easily very young children help others. Children as young as fourteen months interacted with an adult in situations like these:

1. The adult dropped an object from a desk and couldn't easily reach it.
2. The adult, with his hands full of books, was stuck at a cupboard door that he couldn't swing open.
3. The adult couldn't retrieve an object from a closed box, but on the child's side (unknown to the adult) the box was fully open.

In these situations, toddlers show a clear understanding of the adult's (failed) intentions *and* consistently help: They retrieve the toy, they open the cupboard door, and they point to the box's hidden opening. They do this even when they are not praised for it and even when they have to interrupt their own fun activity to help the adult.

Children as young as six months can distinguish someone who helps from someone who hinders, as has been shown in infant violation-of-expectation experiments. Infants look longer when one person hinders instead of helps—they expected helping and gawk at hindering. Slightly older children will actively reward helpers by giving them a hug or a treat but deny those to hinderers.[7]

As Warneken put it, "From an early age human infants and young children are naturally empathic, helpful, generous, and informative." To demonstrate these qualities, a child must understand another's knowledge, intentions, actions, and desires.

But all these understandings are far different in our primate kin. Chimpanzees can partly understand others' intentions, actions, and informational states, especially in a competitive food situation. Yet, chimpanzees rarely help one another, their communication is almost totally imperative, and they try to acquire rather than to inform, help, or cooperate. Theory of mind for primates continues to require a leaner interpretation when it comes to their ability to read minds for cooperation or communication. Communicating, sharing, and helping remain trademarks of being human.*

Or do they?

My Dog Can Read My Mind

Whenever I give talks or classes on theory of mind, a dog owner inevitably says, "My dog reads my mind." I used to be skeptical, thinking that probably a dog became attuned to its owner's cues because the owner provided food, affection, and opportunities for bonding. The true story, however, turns out to be both different and much better.

Research shows that dogs are remarkably good at reading the social and communicative signals of both humans and other dogs. In controlled studies, they easily follow where a person points or where someone is gazing, and they understand the meaning of various words and gestures like *sit, here, ball,* and *Fido.* In addition, they will avoid forbidden food when a watcher's eyes are open but not when they're closed, and they can discriminate between a gaze focused on an object and a gaze focused in space above that object.

Dogs read these social–communicative intentions correctly on the first try, and they show many of these abilities as puppies. Like one-year-old human infants, and unlike even adult chimpanzees, puppies can correctly read points, gestures, and eye gazes; engage in communicative interactions; and otherwise decode the meanings of others. They have taken some steps toward helpful–communicative socialization our primate cousins have not.

To be clear, dogs' social–cognitive skills have limitations. While they pay attention to humans and to human gestures the same way one-year-old infants do, they don't go on to develop the theory-of-mind capacities of even a two-year-old child. Still, they are tuned to humans in a way few other animals are. How did that happen?

---

* To be clear, enhanced human theory-of-mind abilities are not only in the service of helpful–cooperative interactions. Like our primate kin, we also are competitive, selfish animals. And as Jane Goodall noted, we are political ones. Biographies of Josef Stalin often depict him as uncommonly good at reading minds, which may account for his unquestioned success in the social world of political intrigue. After all his crimes, and the incessant vicissitudes of USSR (Union of Soviet Socialist Republics) politics, he still died from natural causes in his bed.

The best hypothesis is that dogs evolved their human-like social prowess through a long history of domestication. In that process, they became less aggressive, less competitive, and less fearful of humans.

Brian Hare, at Duke University, a former student of Mike Tomasello's, is a preeminent dog researcher. His "social–emotional reactivity" hypothesis posits that wild canines (wolves) that were less fearful of and less aggressive toward humans were domesticated over generations.[8] This may have begun as humans tolerated these wolves at their trash dumps, the increased food providing an adaptive advantage for the less fearful–aggressive wolves. Over time and with contact, these canines developed more human-like social–communication capacities. Because canines become reproductively mature in one to two years, 500 years of cohabitation with humans would encompass 200 to 300 generations for canines— plenty of cycles to select for the less aggressive, less fearful temperament Hare hypothesized.

A special breeding study on a Siberian fox-fur farm has reinforced Hare's beliefs. Wild foxes can be aggressive (biting the fur farmers) or fearful (cowering in their cages and not eating well and so not developing healthy coats). To correct these problems, one fur farm began a controlled breeding program. The study was begun surreptitiously in the 1950s because research on genetics and evolution was strictly off limits in Stalinist USSR. Dmitri Belyaev and Lyudmila Trut passed off their experiment as an attempt to breed foxes with more luxurious coats, deemed acceptable since that would improve the Russian economy.

Each generation of fox kits was divided in two. Those that were less fearful of and less aggressive toward their human attendants were bred together. Their kits were tested, and the least fearful and aggressive of that generation were interbred. The other foxes, the control foxes, were bred randomly.

After generations, the target population displays little fear of or aggression toward humans. Unexpectedly, they show other signs of dog-like domestication as well. When kits from this population were tested by Hare on pointing and gaze following, they performed as well as age-matched dog puppies. Control foxes performed poorly on these tests, although they performed as well as domesticated foxes on other tests of nonsocial problem-solving.

Unlike the control foxes, the less fearful, less aggressive experimental foxes like to be held and petted and can live in a home. And, strikingly, they developed floppy ears and pug noses, and they wag their tails, all things that wild foxes never show or do. You can see this on YouTube (search for "Siberian breeding experiment").

Dogs were probably domesticated 20,000 to 35,000 years ago. That domestication resulted in a less aggressive and less fearful temperament, which allowed for better access to human resources. It also facilitated the dogs' better communication, cooperation, and social–cognitive skills, characteristics that make them seem distinctively human. In the process of domestication, dogs also became helpful: They will bring back food to a human, not eating it themselves; they will herd animals; and they become service dogs.[9] All these changes had adaptive value, giving dogs access to humans, their protection, and their resources.

Could our early primate forbearers have evolved in a similar direction, as we domesticated ourselves? Could something like that explain how early primates' competitive, self-centered manipulations gave way to the helpful, communicative theory of mind that is a trademark of humans? Selection against aggression and against fear of humans allowed dogs and foxes to cooperatively coexist with us. It also led to the enhanced theory-of-mind abilities that allow for helpful communications and interactions. Perhaps it did the same for humans. Such a change in temperament and social skills could certainly have given protohumans the advantages of cooperative living: shared food, mutual use of discoveries and inventions, safety in numbers.

Temperamental Humans

So, are we the "domesticated ape"? Did we not only begin to stand upright and use tools, but also change temperament away from incessant primate competition? Was a shift from a highly competitive to a more cooperative social savvy crucial to our evolution and survival?

We can't really know, of course, what provoked our evolution. But, inspired by reading about dog cognition, my colleagues and I realized a human parallel could be tested. Would children who have a more "domesticated" temperament—less aggressive, more helpful, and nonfearful of others—develop better social understanding and social skill than those who don't?

Beginning in infancy, all children show differences in temperament. Some children are more active and restless, while others are more sedate. Some are socially observant; others attend more to objects. Some are aggressive, some "shy," some more cooperative. Temperament in preschoolers has been especially well studied, and we know it influences children's social interactions and social adjustment. These, in turn, could shape a child's theory-of-mind understanding or acquisition. But, what temperament would be most beneficial? A more aggressive child might participate more in social interactions and so gain more experiences that lead to the child developing theory-of-mind insights earlier. Alternatively, the child's aggression might interfere with more sophisticated theory-of-mind understanding, so a reticent but observant child would better understand others and themselves.

We decided to find out.[10] Following the dog-domestication research, we hypothesized that aggressiveness would interfere with a child's theory-of-mind development, while a more socially observant but nonfearful temperament would enhance it.

We assessed almost 150 preschoolers. At age three-and-half, their mothers completed a series of questionnaires about their child's temperament. At three-and-a-half and again at five-and-a-half, the children took theory-of-mind tests, essentially standard preschool false-belief tests. Also, for control purposes, children were given tests for IQ and language abilities.

Temperament at age three-and-a-half clearly predicted theory-of-mind achievements at age five-and-a-half, even when we controlled for other factors. In particular, an aggressive temperament predicted relatively *worse* theory-of-mind development over the next two years, while a shy, but socially observant temperament predicted relatively *better* theory-of-mind development.

The kind of shy, observant temperament that we found to be related positively to theory-of-mind achievement was not fearful, avoidant shyness. These children weren't afraid of others. They were socially interested but observant, as shown on questions like, he or she "prefers to watch first, before joining play" or "is slow to warm up to new people."

In further research of ours, headed by Jonathan Lane, we developed measures to distinguish the two sorts of shyness we thought were often lumped together on most temperament measures. One group included socially withdrawn, fearful–reactive children. The other group included socially reticent children who were low in fearful reactivity. The second group of children liked to look quietly from a distance before joining a social situation, but they were not averse to others. It was the shy but observant, quiet children who showed the best theory-of-mind skills in both the United States and China.

Apparently, too close immersion in the hubbub of activities and emotions can overwhelm a child's social understanding. Nonfearful observation of others can boost it.

These data, along with the dog and chimpanzee findings, convince me that the foundations for our impressive human intelligence are social. The cognitive wherewithal that created print, planes, and iPhones did not originate in the world of objects. The intelligence used to create these things originated in an intelligence used to understand the social world. Indeed, print, iPhones, planes, and many other objects were developed in order to understand and interact within the world of people. I believe our intelligence began as, and is, distinctively social.

Social Intelligence

Nicholas Humphrey, the British evolutionary psychologist I talked about in Chapter 2, said, "The ability to do psychology, however much it might be an ability possessed by every ordinary man and woman, is by no means an ordinary ability."

Humphrey believes our everyday psychology is the foundation for our general intelligence. Humans' increasing mental ability is due to our increasing ability to think about the social world.

His "social intelligence" hypothesis posits that human intelligence arose because protohumans lived in an increasingly complex social world. Those who performed best in the social arena, managing their allies and competitors for instance, lived on. Gradually, the species changed to favor this ability. Humans became more social, and their social life and social reasoning increased. This then prompted further growth in general intelligence.

The social intelligence hypothesis is now also called the "social brain" hypothesis[11] because evidence in its favor has come in part from studying the size of the neocortex in different animals' brains. The neocortex is the convoluted outermost part of the brain that lies closest to the skull. It is particularly large in humans but was more the size of other primates' in early humans. The brain of *Australopithecus*, for example, is about 35 percent the size of the modern human brain, and almost all that difference comes in the size of the neocortex. It is far closer to a chimpanzee brain than to a human one.

Scientists have compared the size of different species' neocortices with their general intelligence. More neocortex is consistently correlated with more intelligence and more learning prowess. This is not a perfect correlation. Several species of birds, especially crows and parrots, are small animals with small brains, yet they have high intelligence. And, all mammals are good at some specialized forms of learning. B. F. Skinner showed that rats have a strong ability to learn with reinforcement conditioning. But, generally, findings are strong: More neocortex means more intelligence, especially more social intelligence.

The neocortex in humans is larger than that of any other mammal*, so, according to the social brain hypothesis, it should indicate increased social intelligence. And, in fact, even children show traits that we might associate with a larger neocortex, like their burgeoning theories of mind. Chimps, our nearest kin, show little of this and also have a smaller neocortex.

Evolutionary anthropologist Robin Dunbar has clarified how much this social intelligence hypothesis is not only about intelligence but also is about learning. Living in complex, close-knit social groups would provide an advantage for those who could track how others might help or harm them. But, this would require learning about a constantly changing environment. Female kin, who protect and aid younger chimps, must leave their natal group at puberty to mate and live elsewhere. Male chimpanzees are more constant geographically, but they form and re-form alliances and hierarchies that shift with age and dominance fights.

So, Dunbar insisted, "If you live in a social world where alliances are important to either your survival or your ability to reproduce successfully, then you must use experience as a guide for your behavior, and this involves learning."

Our human theory of mind reflects beginnings we owe to our nonhuman ancestors. But human theory of mind is distinctive. It is broad, impacting almost all of human cognition and social interaction. It is fundamentally developmental, requiring more and more advanced mind-reading insights over an entire human life. It is also helpful and communicative. Even infants deploy their social–cognitive insights to help, communicate with, and learn about others. While we sprang from animal ancestors, it is our social understanding that makes us uniquely human.

---

* At least it is when balanced with total size and body weight. We have the largest brain-to-body weight ratios.

11

The Social Brain

In a 2006 *New York Times* article,[1] "Cells That Read Minds," Sandra Blakeslee wrote:

> On a hot summer day in Italy, a monkey sat in a special laboratory chair waiting for researchers to return from lunch. Thin wires had been implanted in the region of its brain involved in planning and carrying out movements. Every time the monkey grasped and moved an object, some cells in that brain region would fire, and a monitor would register a sound: brrrrrip, brrrrrip, brrrrrip.
>
> A graduate student entered the lab with an ice cream cone in his hand. The monkey stared at him. Then, something amazing happened: when the student raised the cone to his lips, the monitor sounded—brrrrrip, brrrrrip, brrrrri—even though the monkey had not moved but had simply observed the student grasping the cone and moving it to his mouth.

The research had actually begun with peanuts. Giacomo Rizzolatti, a neuro-scientist at the University of Parma, noticed something strange: Some of the brain cells that fired when a monkey brought a peanut to its mouth also fired when the monkey watched humans or other monkeys bring peanuts to their mouths.

Italian researchers went on to document the phenomenon. The thin wires Blakeslee referred to were so tiny they could record the action of a single neuron in the monkey's brain. They recorded what the researchers called "mirror neurons." These cells, which make up about 20 percent of the cells in one small region of a monkey's motor cortex, had a specialized function. They fired only when a monkey saw bodily movement directed toward a goal: seeing a peanut, no; seeing a mouth open, no; picking up a peanut, yes. And, the monkeys mirror neurons recorded the action in their brains as if they had done the action themself. They allowed the on-looking monkey to

Reading Minds. Henry M. Wellman with Karen Lind, Oxford University Press (2020) © Oxford University Press.
DOI: 10.1093/oso/9780190878672.001.0001

apprehend the action "immediately," automatically. In the *New York Times* article, Dr. Rizollati claimed, "Mirror neurons allow us to grasp the minds of others not through conceptual reasoning but through direct simulation. By feeling, not thinking."

Cells that Read Minds?

This claim that monkey brains could automatically mind-read "by feeling, not thinking" raised enormous interest. It was quickly promoted as a model for understanding humans as well. For example, mirror neuron thinking spawned a short-lived "broken mirror" interpretation for autism. But, testing to determine if humans had mirror neurons was difficult. For ethical reasons, researchers can't implant wires into human brains to measure single cells except in rare medical cases. Instead, most human studies use noninvasive procedures like functional magnetic resonance imaging (fMRI) and event-related potentials (ERPs) to collect data. Sidebar 11.1 describes those techniques and how they measure the activations of thousands or millions of closely packed neurons.

In humans, fMRI studies have shown evidence of specially activated regions of the brain that are used to understand intentional actions. Unlike a monkey's single area for mirroring, the human brain appears to have a network of locations that perform this function. To study mirroring in humans requires the study of entire coordinated brain regions of many, many cells rather than specialized single cells.

Confirmation of these fMRI results came from Dr. Roy Mukamel, now at Hebrew University in Israel, who had a rare opportunity to study single-cell recordings in humans.[2] Twenty-one patients being treated for seizures at the University of California at Los Angeles (UCLA) Medical School were implanted with intracranial electrodes to help control their multiple, intense, and damaging seizures. Thin metal wires were threaded through the cranium and were sited in some targeted cortical cells. His study confirmed fMRI research. Some of the cells appeared to fire identically when actions were either observed or executed, just like the monkeys' did. But in humans, the cells were spread through several neural locations and were part of a wide-ranging system.[3]

Sidebar 11.1. Brief Descriptions of Noninvasive Cognitive Neuroscientific Methods	
Functional Magnetic Resonance Imaging (fMRI)	**Electrophysiology (EEG/ERP)**
- General Description: Uses magnetic pulses around the head to detect changes in blood flow in the brain (an indicator of neural activity because the brain uses oxygen in order to work harder).	- General Description: Uses electrical sensors placed on a participant's scalp to detect the small electrical currents produced by the neurons in the brain when they fire via their electrical–chemical processes (called electrical potentials). This electrical record is a direct result of underlying neural activity and is termed *electroencephalographic* (EEG) data.
- Like an MRI you might have had at a hospital, participants lie surrounded by large magnetic coils that generate magnetic fields. Unlike an MRI (which just detects static anatomy), fMRI detects dynamic activations while the brain is at work. Specifically, it detects changes in oxygen–hemoglobin concentrations in blood flow in the brain.	- Participants sit in an ordinary chair with a special "cap" placed on their head; the cap holds an array of sensors (32, 64, 128 sensors depending on the density of coverage desired). Typically, sensors are evenly spaced around the entire head over the portion where hair grows out of the scalp (of nonbald individuals).
- This neural-dependent blood flow change is termed the *hemodynamic response function*, which peaks about 5 seconds after a neural event.	- A common electrophysiological method is to measure event-related potentials (ERPs). *ERP methods* detect the neural activity associated with processing a particular event (e.g., viewing a target image). The method is used to measure activation patterns across different brief visual or auditory presentations.
- The hemodynamic response function is used to derive the blood oxygen level–dependent (BOLD) signal, which can then be compared across tasks and individuals as an indicator of neural activity.	

Functional Magnetic Resonance Imaging (fMRI)	Electrophysiology (EEG/ERP)
- fMRI has a spatial resolution of about 1–3 mm (given that the magnetic field penetrates deep into the brain to detect blood flow changes very close to the site of neural activity). - Temporal resolution is about 2–5 seconds (given the lag between neural events and their corresponding hemodynamic response). Thus, temporal resolution is much coarser than possible with ERP methods.	- Spatial resolution of EEG data is associated with the number of sensors placed on the head. Thus, it is on the order of centimeters and is always somewhat ambiguous (given several scalp sensors could measure activity from one neural source). Source localization methods that statistically estimate the location of underlying neural sources (via assessment of activity patterns across the scalp sensors and calculations of electrical conductivity of blood, bone, and tissue) can often allow for more precise estimates of the source of the measured brain electrical activity. But regardless, spatial resolution is much coarser than for fMRI. - In compensation, temporal resolution for ERP methods is on the order of milliseconds (given how quickly electrical potentials propagate from the neural source to the scalp surface).

How It Works

Behavioral studies also are being used to shed light on mirroring. Imitation is a common human behavior: Person A taps his hand on a table, and Person B observes the action and then does the same thing. In human adults, imitation is so fast and automatic it suggests to some we may use mirror neurons to perform it. One compelling demonstration of this is what researchers call the *automatic imitation* effect.

In an automatic imitation study, participants tap their right or their left hand, depending on what a model's hands do. The model wears either red or blue gloves, and the imitator can see only their hands. If a model wears blue and taps his or her right hand, imitators are also to tap their right hand. That's the *match* demonstration. But, if the model wears red and taps his or her right hand, imitators are to tap their *left* hand instead—the *mismatch* demonstration. Correct responses are markedly faster for a match demonstration than for a mismatch one. That's the automatic imitation effect: Imitation is so automatic that having to switch hands for a mismatch demonstration derails automatic imitation and either slows the response or leads to error.

The automatic imitation effect suggests direct automatic mapping between action viewing and action performance—a key notion behind mirror neuron thinking. Not surprisingly, the Italian researchers, such as Rizollati, have cited the automatic imitation effect as confirming the presence of mirror neurons in humans.

Does it? And importantly, does the mirror system function from birth, meaning mirror cells are innate? Or, do these cells require substantial learning and development to function indicating a larger mirror system rather than specific mirror neurons? All our current brain data come from adults, adult monkeys and adult humans, so either might be true.

Scientists in Israel were able to exploit a natural experiment to find out.[4] They studied a group of children who had severe cataracts. These children, aged about twelve years, were recent immigrants to Israel from Ethiopia. Their cataracts were uncorrected surgically until they received comprehensive modern healthcare in their new country. Their cataracts allowed enough light into their eyes to allow the children to see light–dark contrasts* but were so severe the children could not see shapes. They could not see hands tapping on tables, for example, until their cataracts were removed.

The children were tested for the automatic imitation effect after their surgeries. For them, the automatic imitation effect was greatly retarded.† This natural experiment suggests two things: First, automatic imitation does not result from innate mirror neurons. It is learned over the course of a person's visual and behavioral development. If perception is impaired early

---

* This was enough for their retinas and visual system to develop normally, so that after their surgeries they had near-normal vision and could recognize hands and colors visually.
† Many of the children were found and tested only well after their surgeries, on average after about eighteen months. This was time enough for some automatic imitation to develop, so the automatic interference effect was not completely missing for them, but clearly it was greatly retarded.

in development, the automatic imitation effect is absent. Second, because automatization is learned, automatic imitation can develop after surgical correction. Most of these children were beginning to learn automatic imitation even though they were older.

Yawning Infects Us

Intriguingly, research on yawning supports a very similar interpretation. You see someone yawn, and a moment later, you find yourself yawning. "It's contagious," you say. And, in fact, it is. Contagious yawning, which activates the mirror system, has evolved fairly recently in humans and monkeys (macaques, baboons, chimpanzees) but in few other species. It is also developmental; contagious yawning (as opposed to spontaneous yawning on your own) does not appear in human infants until the second year of life. It develops with experience.

In fMRI research, contagious yawning—evoked by watching videos of others yawning—activates specific parts of the broadly distributed human imitation system. Brain areas linked to face perception are also activated, but the contagious yawning activations occur in addition to those.[5]

Dogs, with the social–cognitive skills that allow them to attend to and read human gestures and actions, also show contagious yawning: They yawn in reaction to *human* yawns. Dogs yawn more when they see their owners yawn than when they see them open their mouths. And, dogs yawn considerably more when they see their owners yawn than when they see other, unfamiliar humans yawn.

In sum, developmental data from how people and animals develop imitative behavior, like contagious yawning and automatic imitation, do not support hypotheses about innate mirror neurons. Instead, they support the presence of complex, vast, mirroring neural systems that develop slowly over time and experience.

TOMN: The Theory-of-Mind Network

Theory of mind includes, but is much more than, mirroring. What role does the physical brain, including some sort of broad mirror system, play in our human ability to read minds, and how does development influence the process? We know a fair bit about adult brains and minds; most neuroscientific research on theory of mind involves adults. But we have only incomplete and limited answers regarding the development of this ability.

Emerging research with adults shows that theory-of-mind reasoning involves a network of neural regions,[6] as shown in Figure 11.1. These regions are activated when we engage in mental reasoning tasks like the ones I will describe. Activation is impaired in autistic adults. The most consistently activated regions are the medial (that is, middle portion of) prefrontal cortex (PFC), and the right and left temporoparietal junction (TPJ).

In one mental reasoning task, adults tried to infer mental states from photographs of eyes (a theory-of-mind task) while the fMRI tracked blood flow. Blood flow increases to the parts of the brain that are working harder. This is the BOLD (blood oxygen level–dependent) response. When trying to read the mind through the eyes, adults showed increased activation in the medial PFC and in a portion of the temporal lobe (Sidebar 11.1). When those

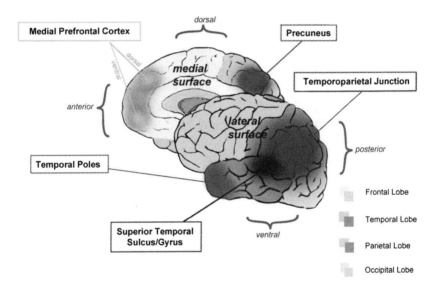

Figure 11.1 The neural regions that comprise the theory-of-mind network. Though shown on only one hemisphere, research demonstrated that most of these regions are activated bilaterally for theory-of-mind reasoning in adults and children.

From Bowman, L. C., & Wellman, H. M. Neuroscience contributions to childhood theory-of-mind development. In O. N. Saracho (ed.), *Contemporary perspectives on research in theories of mind in early childhood education* (pp. 195–223). Charlotte, NC: Information Age, 2014.

same adults were asked to determine a person's gender from the eye photos, those neural sites were not activated.

When this task was adapted to ERP methods (another way to determine brain activity, as outlined in Sidebar 11.1), the results were similar. Adults showed increased activation in frontal scalp locations, roughly corresponding to the PFC, as well as in side scalp locations adjacent to the temporal cortex (over the top of the TPJ).[7]

These same theory-of-mind neural regions are used when adults process descriptions of more complex social interactions and scenes. In one study, adults showed an increased fMRI BOLD response when reading mental state descriptions such as the following:

Rob tied his dog to a lamppost while he went into a store to buy coffee. When he came out, his dog had run across the street. He guessed that the leash had come untied.

In contrast, those regions did not activate if adults read nonmental human descriptions such as this one:

Sheila skipped breakfast because she was late for the train to her mother's. By the time she got off the train, she was starving. Her stomach was rumbling, and she could smell food everywhere.

These sorts of brain fMRI and ERP data have helped identify the sites of the theory-of-mind neural network.

Reasoning about beliefs activates the theory-of-mind neural network as well[8]:

Nicky placed her shoes for that night's prom underneath her dress laid out on her bed. While she was away her sister tried on the shoes and then left them under the bed. Nicky returned to get ready for the prom assuming her shoes were under her dress.

When processing belief-based stories, adults show the BOLD response in the PFC and TPJ. They also show this activation when they attribute true and false beliefs to cartoon characters. In this case, they show more activation when they attribute false beliefs to the characters than when they attribute true ones.

In an ERP study, David Liu, Andy Meltzoff, and I found that when adults reasoned specifically about false beliefs, they showed activation in the scalp regions that correspond to the medial PFC and the right TPJ locations.

These studies, and others, are leading to an emerging consensus: An adult theory-of-mind neural network exists, and it includes multiple sites, especially in the PFC and the TPJ.

Childish Brains

Even if findings from adult studies were crystal clear—and they are not—they would not help us understand children's brains. The brain develops over the course of our lives just as thinking and reasoning do. It is completely possible that adult data would show a theory-of-mind network, while data for children, especially young children, would not. Or, children might show us a theory-of-mind network quite different from the adult one, as children's brains develop along with their developing theory-of-mind understandings. So, we need to study neurocognitive function in children, especially those from ages two to six or seven years, when theory-of-mind changes are pronounced. This research is just beginning.[9] For now, three things can be said:

1. Many of the same sites activated for adult theory-of-mind reasoning *are* activated in children. David Lui, Andy Meltzoff, and I repeated our adult ERP study of false beliefs with children from four to six years of age. Older children who were largely correct on their answers to the false-belief tests showed electrical brain activations that were much like adults'. The activations took longer to unfold (more than a second for children vs. three fourths of a second for adults), but they occurred in the activation sites that roughly correspond to the medial PFC and the right TPJ locations. So, two of the key adult theory-of-mind neural regions—PFC and TPJ—are activated in social–cognitive reasoning in children as well.

2. However, research has also begun to show profound differences between adults and children. The regions recruited for theory-of-mind reasoning change over development. Activations are more diffuse early in life and shift as development proceeds. For example, in our ERP research, compared to older children, younger four-year-olds activated a much bigger portion of frontal sites, and used both left and right

temporal scalp locations (roughly corresponding to left and right TPJ) when they reasoned about false beliefs.

The fMRI technology is not kid friendly, and that limits research with preschoolers. fMRI requires manipulating the magnetic field around the head. The person is inserted into a long, tight tube surrounded by big electromagnets that even adults can find claustrophobic. The process is very noisy; the magnets clatter and rattle loudly. Also, throughout the scan you need to lie very still, or the scan will be blurry and uninformative. You may have experienced some of this for yourself if your doctor has sent you for an MRI scan to help diagnose a knee injury or a possible attack of appendicitis. Few preschoolers can manage all this, so their data—at the age when so many theory-of-mind changes are taking place—rests mostly on ERP.

Even using fMRI with older children requires care, skill, and preparation. Researchers use extra sessions to get the children used to the scanning tube. They provide advanced exposure to the MRI sounds outside the scanner so children know what to expect. They encourage Mom to be present, touching the child's foot while the child is inside the scanner. It is being done, and fMRI is yielding important information about older children's social brain.

3. The theory-of-mind network changes after preschool and into adolescence. Over time, theory-of-mind activations become less diffuse and more specialized. Especially, the right TPJ becomes increasingly specialized to process information about people's beliefs.

The medial PFC is activated during studies that measure mental state reasoning in young children, so are the brain regions corresponding to right and left TPJ areas. But, as children develop, we see increased activation of the right TPJ for belief reasoning and decreased activation of the medial PFC for belief reasoning, which is now used more for reasoning about general mental states.

Developmental changes like these, even if not yet fully mapped or understood, are important because they show neural change. This change would be unlikely if the theory-of-mind network were mature from the start or if theory-of-mind changes after infancy merely reflected exercising that network. Development brings the emergence of a theory-of-mind network and fundamental neural changes in that network.

Plastic Brains

Neuroscience suggests children have a theory-of-mind neural network that uses some of the same neural regions that are used by adults *but* shows considerable change over time. One important task for future research is to disentangle the role of maturational factors from experience in theory-of-mind neural changes.

Mark Sabbagh, who helped me conduct my first developmental neuroscience investigations, explained current neural research: "We are beginning to chart the neural correlates that 'pace' theory-of-mind development." In racetrack terms, if Horse A paces Horse B, it can set the pace from ahead (pulling Horse B along); it can go side by side (in step with Horse B), or it can follow quickly on the heels of Horse B, pushing Horse B along. Given adult data alone, it has been tempting to assume that biologically driven brain maturation "pulls along" improved understanding and performance. But, it could equally be that emerging understandings are pulling brain activations in their wake.

Theory of mind is a deeply developmental achievement, driven by experience and learning. Because the brain is plastic, that experience and learning also shape the structure and the functioning of the brain. We experience and learn new things—faces of friends or math and reading—and the brain changes in response.

Developmental neuroscience increasingly stresses the variety of ways in which brain development is experience-dependent and plastic. Theory-of-mind development also is experience-dependent. Social and cognitive experiences shape both understanding and brain. Theory-of-mind understandings and theory-of-mind brain activations change throughout childhood, together, step by step. There is no simple brain-tells-all story here. We can't say "mirror neurons fire and we automatically read others minds," nor can we say "the brain matures and theory of mind emerges." Mind reading is learned; the social brain is a product of learning as well.

12

Hi, Robot

Eight-year-old Gloria has a robot for a nanny. Robbie protects her, entertains her, and makes sure she is cared for. Her father, George Weston, a robotics engineer, brought Robbie home two years ago. He explained that Robbie is made to be faithful, loving, and kind.

Over the past two years, Gloria and Robbie have become inseparable. She speaks for him, tells him stories, holds his metal hand, and shares secrets and tears with him. She believes Robbie has interests and feelings like a human being, and Gloria would rather play with Robbie than with anyone else. She has come to love Robbie.

But Gloria's mother, Grace, has serious misgivings. "It's Gloria and that terrible machine. You listen to me, George. I won't have my daughter entrusted to a machine—and I don't care how clever it is. It has no soul, and no one knows what it may be thinking." Besides, her mother declares, Gloria won't learn the social skills she needs to interact with humans from "a mess of steel and copper." So, Robbie is sent back to the factory.

This is *Robbie,* the first story in Isaac Asimov's collection, *I, Robot.*[1] The book "revolutionized science fiction and made robots far more interesting than they ever had been," according to the *Saturday Evening Post.* When it was first published in 1950, humanoid robots didn't exist. Today, we see them everywhere: malls, hotels, assembly lines, hospitals, schools, and research laboratories. The 2017 National Robotics Initiative predicted a future when robots will be even more widespread, "as commonplace as today's automobiles, computers, and cell phones. They will be in the air, on land, under water, and in space."[2] But just as Asimov foresaw, some robots definitely make adults uneasy.

The Uncanny Valley

Decades of research show that adults like robots better and better as they become more human-like—up to a point.[3] Once a robot becomes too similar to

Reading Minds. Henry M. Wellman with Karen Lind, Oxford University Press (2020) © Oxford University Press.
DOI: 10.1093/oso/9780190878672.001.0001

a human, it is seen as creepy. We are repelled by robots that look too human or that are too like us in voice, emotion, or even thought. This precipitous drop in liking we experience is called the *uncanny valley*. Figure 12.1 shows two robots that many adults find creepy or uncanny.

You may have experienced this uncanny feeling yourself when you saw or heard robots in movies, in ads, and on YouTube. In the movie *Her,* professional letter writer Theodore (Joachim Phoenix) turns for help to a computer persona, Samantha. Samantha begins to have conversations with Theodore. She has a voice, thoughts, and feelings. Before he can stop himself, a stressed and lonely Theodore falls for Samantha. And, it appears, Samantha reciprocates. Although Samantha has no physical features, viewers see her as definitely human in voice and emotion, and many of us find her creepy and unsettling. We have tumbled into the uncanny valley.

In contrast is the movie *Lars and the Real Girl.* Lars lives in an isolated farming community where there are no unmarried women his age. His

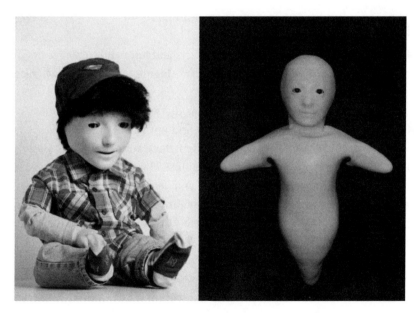

Figure 12.1 This child-like robot (left panel) and Telenoid (right panel) are two robots with human-like features that adults consider unsettling, unnerving, and uncanny according to empirical research.

Right panel: Kaspar image, University of Hertfordshire; Telenoid R1 image: Osaka University and ATR Intelligent Robotics and Communication Laboratories, https://www.roboticstoday.com/institutions/u-of-hertfordshire.

girlfriend is a blowup, life-size sex doll. He brings her to social engagements, introduces her to his friends, and appears to have a life with her, although she has no thoughts, emotions, or speech. Viewers have called *Lars and the Real Girl* "utterly charming," "touching," and a "film that believes in simple human kindness." Lars's girlfriend is acceptable to us (and to Lars's friends in the film) because, although she has some human features, she is not too closely human.

Some scientists think we find very human-like robots creepy because we have evolved a fear of illness, and these robots look or sound like sick people. Others argue that human-like robots give the impression they can think and feel, but we, as adults, don't believe machines should be able to do those things. We become unsettled when they look, act, or sound like they can.

Asimov's portrayal of Grace Weston foreshadowed an uneasiness with robots scientists discovered only decades later. Was his portrayal of Gloria's love of Robbie equally accurate?

Creepiness Creeps In

Robots alleged to appeal to, play with, teach, and tutor children have flooded the marketplace in the past dozen years. Figure 12.2 shows five recent additions.

But no research showed if these robots did what they promised. My colleague Kimberly Brink and I wanted to find out what attracted or repelled, worked or didn't work, with the children these robots were supposed to help.[4] Over two years, we interviewed almost 250 children, from ages three through eighteen, about their beliefs and feelings about three different robots: a very human-like robot (left in Figure 12.3) and a parallel machine-like robot (right in Figure 12.3), plus the NAO robot shown in the top left of Figure 12.2.

It turned out that children younger than nine years, like Gloria but unlike adults, didn't think human-like robots were creepy at all. (And they really liked NAO.) This means it's unlikely adults find human-like robots creepy because the robots evoke our evolved aversion to sick humans. If that were true, even very young children would find them creepy.

But at about age nine, the children's reaction to robots changed. After that, the uncanny valley reaction emerged, and children found a notably human-like robot much creepier than a machine-like robot.

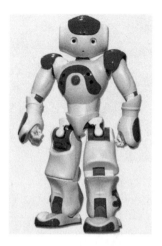

Figure 12.2 NAO robot in top left panel; Robovie (top right); iPal (bottom left panel); Jibo (bottom center); and Zenbo (bottom right) are all robots with features and behaviors designed specifically for interacting with children.

Top panel, left to right: NAO image: SoftBank Robotics; Robovie image: Vstone and Advanced Telecommunications Research Institute International (ATR). Bottom panel, left to right: iPal image: Nanjing AvatarMind Robot Technology; Jibo image: Jibo, Inc.; Zenbo image: Asus.

This seems to happen because children's sense of what a mind is or can do and what machinery is or can do, changes. Eight-year-old Gloria and her peers are happy to believe robots can see, hear, think, play, and cry. They *prefer* a robot that does those things because it seems comfortingly familiar and because that kind of robot can be their friend and can protect them. For young children, the more mind the better. For older children and adults, the more a robot seems to have a mind, especially a mind that gives rise to human-like feelings and thoughts, the *creepier* it becomes.

Figure 12.3 Closely human-like robot on left and a machine-like counterpart on right (shown from back so participants could see its machinery). Video clips of each robot showed the robot moving its head from side to side.

From K. A. Brink, K. Gray, & H. M. Wellman, Creepiness creeps in: Uncanny valley feelings are acquired in childhood. *Child Development, 90,* 1202–1214, 2017. [Epub ahead of print] doi:10.1111/cdev.12999.

What changes around age nine to ten? The most likely explanation is that children begin to understand and separate the concepts of mind, brain, and body. As I described in Chapter 8, children begin to see the mind as more "mental," and the biological brain as a part of the body that houses the mind. Machines such as robots aren't biological, so they shouldn't house human minds. The uncanny valley results when they seem to do so.

So, Asimov's portrait of Gloria, who turns eight as *Robbie* unfolds and whose character and reactions drive the story, was prescient. It is fiction, but it is not pure fantasy.

Hi, Robot.

Learning from Robots

Jim and Kerry Kelly live in a small town in the rural Midwest. Their sons, Ben, five, and Ryan, twelve, attend the local public school. Their school district is always short staffed. The closest town is forty miles away, and pay for teachers is abysmal. And, even the best school districts struggle to find teachers. Nationally, over the past ten years, teacher training programs have declined in enrollment, and 50 percent of new teachers leave the profession within their first five years. None of this has helped Pleasantville.

This year, the district's staffing has hit a critical low: Class size will have to be huge, and there's limited money for aides who might help with the teaching load, which will further discourage teacher applications. The school board considers accepting underqualified teachers. Parents are up in arms. Teachers and principals are stressed. The situation comes to a head at a school board meeting that drags on past midnight with shouting, frustration, threats, and anger. But, it's too important to back off: Children's futures are at stake.

In the next week, the superintendent finds a possible solution. The state has money available to help school boards implement technology in qualified districts. Pleasantville qualifies. They can receive funds to buy robots to serve in the classrooms. The robots can assume some of the teaching load, improve teaching quality, and relieve the overcrowding.

Ten years ago, this would have been unthinkable. Soulless machines educating our children? But solutions are few, and the superintendent has found reports of success from other schools. He sells his plan well, and against all expectations, the school board agrees. The following fall, the Kelly kids, like all the kids in the district, have a robot in the classroom.

At the half-year mark, the school board reviews their decision. In six-year-old Ben's class, the results are outstanding. Kids learn fast—pretty much as fast from the robot as from the human teacher. And, the kids like the interactions with the machines. The teacher can accomplish more and is less stressed in the process. Everyone is pleased.

But Ryan's class, at age eleven, has a far different experience. The robot used in their class is identical to the one in Ben's class—very human-like. By January, the kids hate it. They call it names; they hit it; they learn little from it. It sits in a corner, scorned by students and teacher alike.

Like Asimov's, this scenario is fiction, but it reflects the real world. Many school districts are hurting for staff, and robots are entering the classroom. In Korea, Robosem teaches English to children, and in the United States, RUBI teaches Finnish. Child-like robots, including NAO, are helping autistic children practice social interactions through imitation games, turn taking, and conversation. Ursus, a large robotic bear, administers physical therapy to children with motor disorders like cerebral palsy.

Trustworthy Testimony

Using robots as teachers makes some sense. Children learn much of their knowledge from others: parents, teachers, peers. Children trust that 8 ×

8 = 64, that Earth is round, and that dinosaurs are extinct, not because they have uncovered these facts themselves but because reliable sources have told them so. Research shows that children are adapted to learn general knowledge from human communication. The phenomenon is known as "trust in testimony."

But, do children trust the testimony of robots? Does it matter if the robot behaves, responds, or even looks like a human? If children learn from a robot, do they learn in the same way they learn from a human teacher? Excellent questions.

Research shows that when children as young as preschool age learn from other people, they monitor their informants' knowledge, expertise, and confidence. They remember whether a person has given them accurate information in the past. They also monitor an informant's access to information: Did she see the thing she is telling me about? They attend to the person's qualifications: Is he a knowledgeable adult or a naïve child? And, they monitor a person's confidence or uncertainty about their answers: Did she say she *knows* it or *thinks* it?

Surprisingly little is known about how and if children learn from robots. Because robots are machines, children could see them as infallible, like calculators or electronic dictionaries. If so, they might accept any information from a robot without considering if it is accurate. Or, children might see robots as a more fallible machine: a toaster that burns the toast, Siri that can give wrong or even outlandish answers, or an alarm clock that goes off in the middle of the night. If so, they might resist a robot's teachings.

Kim Brink and I researched these questions.[5] First, we studied three-year-olds, an age when children learn well and judiciously from human teachers in standard trust-in-testimony research. You can see the setup in Figure 12.4.

In the first phase of our study, Kim asked two different colored NAO robots to name four familiar objects. The robots looked and pointed at objects like a teddy bear or a ball. One robot correctly named all four, while the other incorrectly named all four (for example, it called the teddy bear "a tree"). Then, Kim asked children an "Accuracy Check" question: Which robot was not very good at answering questions?

Following that, Kim presented four new, unfamiliar, objects (for example, one was a garlic press) and asked the children which robot they would like to ask for the name. This is the "Ask" question.

Each robot then gave a different, made-up, name for each object. For a garlic press, one said, "It's a modi," and the other said, "It's a toma." Kim then

Figure 12.4 This is a still frame from the video of an initial study to investigate whether children appropriately trust (and mistrust) the testimony of social robots. The NAO robot on the left is white plastic with orange markings; the NAO on the right is white with purple markings.

asked what the child thought was the correct name of the object, a modi or a toma. That's the "Endorse" question. Basically, it asks if the children trust or mistrust information from each robot.

These preschoolers did, in fact, track which robot was accurate and which was not on the Accuracy Check question. Further, they trusted the testimony of the more accurate robot. On the Ask questions, they overwhelmingly said they wanted to ask the accurate robot what this new thing was called. On the Endorse questions, the children overwhelmingly said the name for the object was the name provided by the accurate robot. These young children accurately learned new words (albeit words we made up) from robots. In fact, these young children learned from the accurate robot at the same rate they learned from an accurate human.

We also asked the children their beliefs about the NAO robots' minds. Could these robots "think for themselves," "decide what to do," or "feel fear"? The preschoolers generally answered yes to at least one of these questions. But, some said the NAOs could think for themselves, decide what to do, and be afraid. Others said they could do only one or two of those things.

When asking for names, preschoolers who saw the robots as having more mind (who gave more yes answers) were more likely to choose the accurate robot over the inaccurate one than were children who attributed less mind to the robots. Those children who saw the robots as having more mind were also significantly more likely to learn the name for the object when it was given by the accurate robot.

Young children clearly can and do learn from robots, and they are appropriately choosy about the sort of robot teachers they accept.

Developing Ideas About Robots

Most research on robots and children involves a single age group in a single study with a single type of robot, so results haven't been comprehensive. But, if we amass data from these very different studies, we can get some idea of the wider developmental picture.[6]

How Younger Children Learn from Robots

Interactive robots seem to be more effective teachers for three- to six-year-olds than information-spouting ones. Three- to six-year-olds were more likely to ask for information and agree with a robot that responded to them rather than to one that just reported information. When learning new vocabulary words, toddlers were more likely to attend to an interactive human-like robot instructor than they were to an inanimate audio speaker. Japanese four- to six-year-olds performed better when a robot used a teaching style that required the children to interact with it as a team member.

Children this age learned best from a robot when that robot's voice, appearance, or behavior resembled that of a human. When a robot taught children the functions and locations of different utensils in a table-setting task, children who learned from a robot with a human-like voice recalled more on later tests than children who learned from the exact same robot that had a machine-like voice.

Young Korean children learned English better from an interactive robot that could emote, sing, talk, and dance compared to a noninteractive computer or textbook with identical instructional material.

What about older children?

Younger Versus Older Children and Robots

In the table-setting task, four- to six-year-olds improved dramatically when taught by the human-voiced robot. After their robot training, they performed on a par with seven- to ten-year-olds. When seven- to ten-year-olds received the same training from the same robot, they showed only minimal improvement, and for them the voice of the robot, whether robotic or human-like, made no difference.

In other research, children in a range of ages engaged in classroom tasks with a robot that seemed mindful; for example, it learned the child's name or appeared to stop to think reflectively. The younger children learned more from the mindful robot than children who engaged with a robot that was equally informative but wasn't mindful. A mindful robot did not enhance the learning of older children.

In a Japanese study, the robot Robovie (shown in Figure 12.2) traveled around a Japanese school to speak English with first graders (six- to seven-year-olds) and sixth graders (eleven- to twelve-year-olds). This robot performed interactive, mindful behaviors like hugging, shaking hands, playing rock–paper–scissors, singing, briefly conversing, and pointing at nearby objects. First graders spent significantly more time interacting with the robot than sixth graders did.

In our uncanny valley research, young children attributed myriad human-like qualities to robots. They believed that robots could have emotional, social, and perceptual abilities like sight and touch. That finding has appeared in other research as well. Three- and five-year-olds claimed that a robot dog, very like AIBO (shown in Figure 12.5), could see and be tickled. They said the dog could also think and be happy.

As you might now predict, children's expectations that robots have emotional and perceptual capacities *decrease* as they age. Eight-year-olds, but not fifteen-year-olds, reported that a three-foot-tall interactive Robovie could be intelligent, have interests, and experience emotions.

When Japanese researchers asked children about robots, children younger than seven often spoke of them in human-like terms. Robots were "he" or "she," not "it," and they were said to have autonomous actions or desires. As children grew older than seven, they more often used the same pronouns for robots they used for inert man-made machines.

Figure 12.5 Machine-like robots that differ in body type: one kangaroo-like, one dog-like, and one roughly human-like. Left to right: BionicKangaroo (image: Festo); AIBO ERS-7 (image: Sony); Robovie Nano Robot (made from a kit).

Top panel left to right: BionicKangaroo (Image: Festo); AIBO ERS-7 (Image: Sony); Robovie Nano Robot (made from a kit) (image: Vstone, https://www.japantrendshop.com/robovie-nano-robot-kit-p-3945.htm).

Young children, like Gloria in the Asimov story, accept some robots with the same delight and fearlessness they show toward household pets. When I was beginning my research on children and robots, a research assistant brought her four-year-old son, Alex, to my lab for a visit. Alex saw parts of two studies. In one laboratory room, we had a small friendly dog, Fiona, interacting with children. In another laboratory room, we had a NAO robot.

Alex was immediately attracted to Fiona, fearlessly approaching and petting her. Strikingly, he had a similar reaction to NAO. He was intrigued and then interacted when Nao looked at his face with lit-up eyes and learned his name.

As our uncanny valley research showed, as children age, they begin to think robots are more like machines than people. Older children expect that robots are only capable of some forms of thinking and decision-making; they don't believe they can be tickled or feel fear. Neither do we adults.

Feelings Toward Robots

Before the creepiness of the uncanny valley sets in, robots can offer many benefits for children. Younger children have told researchers that some in-home robots, like AIBO the robot dog, could make them feel safe if they were home alone with it. Other young children have said that even a thoroughly metallic robot, like the one in Figure 12.5, could be a friend they would feel comfortable sharing secrets with. Three- to nine-year-old children who believed that Robovie could have interests and experience emotions also believed that Robovie could be their friend and could comfort them if they were sad. When receiving injections at a hospital, children with severe anxiety were comforted more by a playful NAO robot than by a human nurse.

Like Gloria in Asimov's story, these young children easily developed positive feelings toward robots, while older children and adults easily developed feelings that were more negative.

Morality for Robots?

Isaac Asimov's book, *I, Robot*, is primarily about morality and robotics: how robots interact with humans for good or evil. Most of the stories revolve around the efforts of Dr. Susan Calvin, chief roboticist for the fictional U.S. Robotics and Mechanical Men, Incorporated, the primary producer of advanced humanoid robots in the world. She worries about aberrant behavior of advanced robots, and she develops a new field, *robopsychology*, to help figure out what is going on in their electrical ("positronic") brains.

All robots produced by U.S. Robotics and Mechanical Men are meant to be programmed with the "Three Laws of Robotics":

1. A robot may not injure a human being or, through inaction, allow a human being to come to harm.
2. A robot must obey the orders given it by human beings except where such orders would conflict with the First Law.
3. A robot must protect its own existence as long as such protection does not conflict with the First or Second Laws.

But in Asimov's stories, flaws are found in the robots and their prototypes. These lead to robots imploding, harming people, and in one key case, killing a man.

Asimov's *I, Robot* stories have spawned numerous spinoffs, continuations, and commentaries. A 2004 episode of *The Simpsons* (titled "I, D'oh Bot") featured a robot boxer named Smashius Clay. Smashius, self-defeatingly, follows all of Asimov's three laws and loses to every human he fights.

The Twentieth Century Fox 2004 film, *I, Robot,* starred Will Smith as detective Dell Spooner of the 2035 Chicago police department. Dell investigates a murder of the roboticist Dr. Alfred Lanning, which may have been at the hand of a robot. The movie named Asimov's Three Laws of Robotics as part of its plot line.

Currently, robots like NAO, Robovie, and Kaspar don't have moral codes programmed in. But then, as yet they also don't have anything like full positronic machine intelligence. Conversely, we don't have laws or codes about how to treat robots. For example, should a really human-like robot have rights? In November 2017, the Kingdom of Saudi Arabia granted a robot, Sophia, citizenship. Sophia is the robot on the left in Figure 12.6. This set off an uproar about rights among women in Saudi Arabia. For example, Saudi women must veil their faces when they are in public; Sophia appeared in public and on TV without a veil.

Researchers, robot designers, parents, and teachers have become increasingly concerned that interactions with robots will promote antisocial behaviors.[7] A hitchhiking robot successfully traveled around Germany, Canada, and the Netherlands, taking pictures and carrying on conversations with other travelers. It was vandalized and destroyed after several weeks in the United States. A mall security robot designed to share information with customers routinely faced abuse from unsupervised children. They would kick and push the robot. And, it's easy to imagine a "posthuman" world when robots displace humans from jobs and so are attacked and sabotaged by

Two Very Human-like Robots and One Person

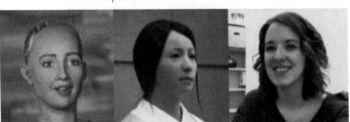

Figure 12.6 Two very human-like robots and one person. Sophia, who was granted Saudi Arabian citizenship (left panel); Actroid, a robot used in Japan (center panel); and a real person (right panel).

Left to right: Sophia image: Hanson Robotics.com; Actroid F image: Kokoro Company Ltd.; Dr. Brink self-photo.

those they've displaced. This is already a theme for science fiction novels and movies. In nonfiction, the *New York Times* recently published an article on the topic, "How to Robot-Proof Your Child."[8]

Empirical research suggests that antisocial behaviors toward robots can be reduced, in part, by modifying the robots.[9] Preschool children in a classroom comforted a robot with a hug and protected it from aggression when it started to cry after being damaged or played with too roughly. At least one study has shown that younger children say a robot should be treated fairly and should not be psychologically harmed after having conversed and played with the robot for fifteen minutes.

Into the Future

Every year, robots become a larger part of our lives and the lives of our children. Look again at Figure 12.2 to see Pixar-like robots that have been manufactured in the last few years. They are designed to play games, answer questions, read stories, and even watch children unsupervised. Current research suggests robots might be effective in these roles with younger children but less so with older ones. Because robots play an expanding role in children's lives, we need an expanding research program to understand child–robot interactions for children in a wide range of ages.

Further studies are also needed to examine children's learning from robots, along with the complex relationship between children's perceptions of robots, how they treat them, and how those interactions impact children's social and moral development and their interactions with others.

This is not research that can be done once, today, with the results guaranteed for tomorrow. We will need to discover how tomorrow's children, who may grow up with robots as a constant fixture of their lives, think and interact with them. Children born during the Depression grew up to have different perspectives than those born during World War II or in the 1950s. Today's young children may look at robots quite differently from current adults because of their vastly different experiences with them.

Conceivably, one day the uncanny valley could disappear. As human-like robots become more commonplace, older children and adults may expect that robots, although machines, *can* look surprisingly human and *do* have minds that encompass many human-like experiences. One day, even highly human-like robots may seem comfortingly familiar—*or not*. It remains to be seen. Just as it remains to be seen how our increasing contact with robots will impact our everyday theory of mind and how it develops.

13

Theory of Mind at Work

Theory of mind is at work all around us. It is a foundation for our human way of looking at the world, so whether false or true, whether directed at ourselves or at others, it colors our thinking, our institutions, and our basic beliefs.

At Work in the Law

March 22, 1960, saw the start of a murder trial at the Finney County courthouse in Garden City, Kansas. Two men were accused of killing a local farmer, his wife, and two children in a burglary that netted them $25 each. The trial lasted only seven days; the jury deliberated only forty-five minutes before returning a verdict of guilty. Both men were sentenced to death as mandated for first-degree murder at that time in Kansas.

The murderers, Richard Hickock and Perry Smith, were recent parolees from the Kansas State Penitentiary. Their victims were Herb Clutter; his wife, Bonnie; daughter, Nancy (age 15); and son, Kenyon (14). The murders took place early Sunday morning, November 15, 1959, in the prosperous Clutters' farmhouse.

Hickock and Smith were apprehended soon after the murders. Floyd Webber, a former cellmate of Hickock's who had once been a hand at the Clutters' farm, contacted the prison warden. He said Hickock had planned to rob Clutter and to "leave no witnesses." Armed with that tip, Hickock and Smith were arrested six weeks later in Las Vegas. They confessed to the murders and were brought back to Kansas for trial. Their plan was based on a false belief: Hickock thought Clutter had $10,000 hidden in a safe in his house—not so.

The Hickock–Smith trial passed unnoticed by most Americans outside Kansas, and both men were executed by hanging on April 14, 1965, after almost five years on death row. Just months later, however, Hickock and Smith

Reading Minds. Henry M. Wellman with Karen Lind, Oxford University Press (2020) © Oxford University Press.
DOI: 10.1093/oso/9780190878672.001.0001

were two of the most famous murderers in twentieth-century America. Their crime was the subject of Truman Capote's *In Cold Blood*, published in the spring of 1966.[1] *In Cold Blood* was arguably the first true crime book published. It became an instant success, and today is the second-best-selling true crime book in publishing history, behind only Vincent Bugliosi's *Helter Skelter* about the Manson murders. It has been adapted for film and was the basis of a TV miniseries.

In the Judeo–Christian tradition, "Thou shalt not kill" is one of the Ten Commandments God handed down to Moses. The Q'ran declares murder a sin; prohibitions against murder are part of almost all moral and legal systems. At the same time, legal scholars and moral considerations argue that, while the perpetrators must be culpable for their crimes, they should not be punished more than they deserve. In the case of homicide, this involves layered distinctions.

Laws about murder in the United States, Canada, Australia, and New Zealand have historical roots in English common law. This states that for someone to be at fault for a crime, *actus reus non facit reum nisi mens sit rea*. That is, "the mind must recognize the crime for the perpetrator to be guilty." Culpability rests not only on the physical act (someone dies at the hands of another) but also, crucially, on the actor's relevant mental state (does the killer act with knowing intent). *Actus reus* requires **mens rea**.

Hickock and Smith were hanged for first-degree premeditated murder. Hickock planned the burglary while he was still in jail, and a part of his plan was to leave no witnesses. In basic think–want theory of mind terms: Hickock engaged in an *act* he *thought* would get him what he *wanted*. *Mens rea* is saturated with think–want psychology.

Most countries divide homicide into several categories of murder and manslaughter. To help systematize distinctions that differed widely by state and locale, the American Law Institute published the Model Penal Code (MPC) in 1962.[*,2]

The MPC sets out several levels of culpability, all dependent on the perpetrator's state of mind. The most stringent level involves murder done "purposefully." The perpetrator's conscious intent is to cause death. On the testimony of three medical doctors, the judge ruled that Smith and Hickock

---

* The MPC, last updated in 1981, is advisory; it guides state legislatures to update their penal codes but has no force of law on its own. Most states have adopted part, but not all, of its practices and definitions.

were mentally able: They *knew* what they were doing and that it was un-lawful, but acted anyway because they *wanted* to leave no witnesses: think–want psychology.

The penal code also defines lesser crimes, such as *"knowing" homicide*: The perpetrator might not specifically intend to cause death but does intend to inflict a level of harm that would clearly be likely to cause death. For example, John Doe intends to beat Jane to unconsciousness, and she dies as a result of the beating. *Reckless homicide* is less intentional still: The perpetrator acts "recklessly," disregarding the law with a high risk of causing death. John fires a gun in a crowd, not intending to kill anyone but doing so. *Accidental homicide* is the least purposeful act: A death occurs without intent: Jane is traveling at the speed limit when someone races in front of her car, is run over, and dies.

Theory-of-mind thinking provides us with legal distinctions like these. The terms—premeditation, reasonable doubt, knowing intent, state of mind—have specific legal meanings, but we easily understand those meanings because they spring from commonsense psychology. They are all notions within our broader think–want reasoning. Our moral reasoning grows from this same mens rea foundation. Actions are good or bad according to the intentions behind them. Harming your neighbor's flower bed may be regrettable no matter how it happens, but it is only reprehensible if you do it on purpose.

Mind Bubbles Up

Remember those superheroes who debuted in comic books: Superman, Iron Man, Wonder Woman, Wolverine? They tell us about themselves using thought bubbles. On the surface, those are curious devices: thought made pictorial. But we understand them. Here too theory of mind works for us; in this case, it makes natural a potentially strange device.

Reading seems similarly natural to mature readers. But reading is an unnatural act. While verbal language comes readily to humans, reading is the product of arduous learning. Print, which depicts fleeting sounds as permanent marks on a page, took millennia and generations to invent, and it cropped up independently in only a few locales in human history: in the middle east, China, and Central America. Reading initially befuddles many children and can take years to understand and master.

Pictorial conventions, which might seem more universal, turn out to take effort and training as well and have been honed over generations. How a culture renders dynamic action on a static surface provides a telling example and varies widely in different cultures and across history. Ancient Egyptians are depicted walking with the top of the body facing the viewer, while the hips and legs are skewed an impossible 90 degrees to face the direction of travel. Cave paintings used special (sometimes curious) postures to depict animals running. Ancient Hawaiians' drawings of surfing had their own peculiarities. Conventions were required to produce, read, and then perfect these depictions.

Comic book artists developed or borrowed another set of conventions. Action lines stream out behind a static forward-leaning person to show running, or marks emanate from someone's mouth to depict sound. Research that has tested children's understanding of comic book conventions shows that children don't understand these depictions of action or noise until six to nine years of age.

Are our superheroes' thought bubbles conventions we understand only after training or enculturation? That seems likely because, recall, even three-year-olds say that thoughts are invisible and immaterial, but thought bubbles depict thoughts in clearly visible, tangible terms—a picture on paper.

Further, thought bubbles are rarely used in picture books for preschoolers, while they're common in the comic books written for their older siblings. When my colleagues and I surveyed more than 200 preschool picture books from the United States, Spain, England, and Japan, less than 3 percent of the books had thought bubbles. This suggests that writers for children believe preschoolers need training to understand this convention, the way they need training to understand print.

But what if thought bubbles were obvious, even to children? Conceivably, once preschoolers understand mind, with its thoughts and ideas, they could understand that its workings could be depicted. If so, this would show us a previously unknown way theory of mind works in our world, and at an early age.

In our research,[3] we discovered that young three-year-olds understood thought bubbles almost immediately. We showed children a picture like Figure 13.1, pointed at the thought bubble, and said, "This shows what he is thinking." Young children could then easily and accurately go on to answer questions like, "What is he thinking about?" (saying "wagon" not "dog," even though the boy is equally connected to both). Better than 85 percent of

Figure 13.1 Thought bubble depiction of a boy thinking about a wagon.

three-year-olds could do this for the initial pictures as well as for subsequent pictures where we said nothing about the thought bubble and simply asked what the character was thinking.

Young children quickly "read" thought bubbles. Can they go further? Can they understand that thought bubbles depict others' subjective experiences? Yes.

We showed preschoolers two cardboard paper dolls, a boy and a girl, who look into a dark box. When the boy was turned over, the child saw he had a thought bubble of a doll. When the girl was turned over, she had a thought bubble of a teddy bear. These preschoolers easily answered, "What does the boy think is in the box?" (doll), and "What does the girl think is in the box?" (teddy bear). They understood from the thought bubbles that the boy and the girl had different thoughts. Even three-year-olds were 90 percent correct on these thought bubble tests.

Three- and four-year-olds can also pass other, related, tests. They say pictures show something a person can see and touch, while thought bubbles show something a person cannot see and touch, even though both are shown as pictures on paper. Children, like adults, find thought bubbles to be an easy and clear-cut way to depict invisible, subjective thoughts. They're natural.

Some ways of thinking and learning are natural, intuitive, easy; some are unnatural, counterintuitive, and hard. Theory of mind is at work here. It naturalizes some surprising parts of our life, even some, like thought bubbles, that have only recently been invented. Mind bubbles up.

Mysteries of Mind

Mysteries rivet us, a truth that begins in childhood. In one of our studies, an adult showed preschoolers two kinds of blocks that might light up special boxes when they were placed on top of them.[4] The blue cubes consistently lit up the light boxes ("It's a starter"); the red pyramids consistently did not ("It's a do-nothing").

For the test trial, two light boxes were set side by side, and the adult placed a blue cube on one and simultaneously placed a red pyramid on the other. *Both* blocks lit up their boxes. The adult waved her hand vaguely in the direction of the boxes and asked, "Why did that happen?"

The children had a choice. Either they could choose to explain the easier phenomenon, why the starter lit up its box ("It's a starter," "those always work"). Or, they could choose the more difficult explanation, why the do-nothing now works. Overwhelmingly, they tried to explain why the do-nothing now, surprisingly, worked. It was a mystery, and their explanations attempted to decode the mystery: "Maybe, that one just looks like a do-nothing but really it's a starter." "Before you didn't put it on hard enough; I bet do-nothings work too if you really push 'em down hard."

TV and podcast producers know the power of mystery. Crime and whodunits are the most watched adult genre after sports. Who did what and why, are, of course, theory-of-mind questions.

Child audiences find a mystery equally entrancing. *Blue's Clues* is a great example. *Blue's Clues* follows an animated blue dog (Blue) as she leaves a set of clues for humans Steve (or Donovan) and child viewers to follow.[5] Typically, each show has four to eight mysteries: It's Blue's birthday, what will Steve get her? Blue disappears and leaves a footprint; Steve puts Blue's present in a wrapped box, but then loses it among a lot of similar boxes. At each juncture clues mount up, and Steve asks one or more key questions ("What does Blue really like?" "Which box has my present?"). And then he waits. And after a long pause, Steve provides a hint or two.

During the pauses, children shout out answers. Or at least they do late in the week. *Blue's Clues* airs the exact same episode each day for a week. Early in the week young children need all the hints, and they need to watch Steve decode the clues. Later in the week, after watching several times, children gleefully shout out the answers at each pause. Each week, *Blue's Clues* declares mysteries, then solves them by following clues—again, and again, and again.

Mysteries revolve around ignorance, solving them turns ignorance and guesses into knowledge—that's theory-of-mind thinking. *Blue's Clues* is based on theory-of-mind research about children, including how children read a person's intentions, thoughts, feelings, mistakes, errors, and ignorance. And, the show has inspired research about how effective it is as a learning tool (very).

Theory of Mind at Work for Childish Adults

Meditative practices around the world encourage us to live in the moment and to cultivate a child-like mind of awe and compassion. It's not easy to do; we're distracted by worries, by plans, by schedules. It takes work. But, a child-like mindset is one of the many ways theory of mind can work for us. It gives us a ready-made channel that allows us to tap into this fundamental source of joy and wonder.

This is just one way out of many that theory of mind can and does link our self of today with the child we once were.

Theory of Mind Works Against Us

Our theory of mind works for us when adults understand the law, children understand thought bubbles, and all of us pursue mysteries. It is, without doubt, one of the most powerful tools for understanding at work in our lives. But equally, it trips us up. It leads us to missteps and false approaches, even in areas where we'd swear we're expert.

Forecasting Feelings

Imagine winning the lottery. Would you feel happy or sad? How happy do you think you'd feel on a scale where 1 is unhappy and 7 is extremely happy? How happy would you feel the day your jackpot is announced? How happy would you feel six months later?

While adults are good at correctly predicting they'd feel happy, they consistently overestimate how happy they'd feel. For the day they hear they won, they correctly predict they'd feel very happy. But after that, their accuracy drops. Real lottery winners' happiness quickly subsides. A month after winning, they are usually no happier than before they won, and sometimes they are a lot *less* happy. Few people predict that.[6]

This poor affective forecasting happens all the time. Adults of all ages overestimate how unhappy they'll be three months after the breakup of a romantic relationship. College professors underrate how they'll feel a few years after being denied tenure. Hopeful mothers-to-be overrate how unhappy they'll be a week after receiving a negative pregnancy test.

We all over- and underpredict our future feelings.

A key reason for this is our ever-active, theory-of-mind drive to explain human events. When something unusual happens, we spend a lot of time attempting to make sense of it: "I thought I was so in love; I wonder why I don't feel so bad now it's over?" "I was sure if I won the lottery I'd be on top of the world, why aren't I?"

Our theory-of-mind reasoning helps us come up with sensible explanations: "It was just infatuation." "Lottery wins are not as huge as they want you to believe, after the IRS takes a big bite and your prize gets dribbled out over years." By making sense of events, people normalize them. Your reactions seem more inevitable and normal once you've puzzled them out, so they become less emotionally fraught. But no one predicts that ahead of time.

Our errors in affective forecasting reflect flaws in our everyday theories about emotions and their timing. Although we constantly experience emotions, we're far from expert about them.*

Surprise: It's Not the Thought that Counts

The quest to come up with the perfect surprise gift gets great press. Christmas, Valentine's Day, and Mother's Day ads depict its rewards. But we're not that great at forecasting what someone else wants. Striving for the

---

* Theory-of-mind thinking suggests some things to do. First, don't undercut your own good feelings when they occur. Savor them, knowing they may not last all that long. At the same time, don't overreact to initial bad feelings. You will feel better with time and often with less time than you feared. And, don't undervalue normal in search of bigger, headier pizzazz. Being mildly happy often, rather than really, really happy occasionally, has a lot to recommend it. Fortunately, most adults say they're mildly happy often. Enjoy it.

big surprise often results in a failure. Sometimes, you buy a gift the person doesn't want. But, even when your gift gets a great reaction initially, it often has no long-term appeal. It languishes in a dusty closet, basement, or drawer, unused. Research by Jeff Galak at Carnegie Mellon has shown this indisputably.[7]

Fortunately, there's an easy remedy. "The single best thing that gift givers can do is to ask recipients what it is they want," Galak said. "The problem is that in our culture, it is taboo to do so. Somehow it seems like by asking what someone wants, it makes you, the giver, seem less thoughtful. This just isn't true. Gift recipients are happier with *requested* gifts because they are the things that they actually want."

We get into trouble here because, while we read minds all the time, it's hard for us to get the details exactly right. It's especially hard to read people's minds about their desires. You know better what *you* want and will use than anyone else, and that's true for others as well. Study after study by Galak and others shows it's better just to ask. Asked-for gifts are sources of deeper and more long-lasting pleasure. Give the gift of asking.

Easy Knowledge Is Bad for You

Our everyday beliefs about learning and remembering also lead us astray. This is true even for college students who must have adequate learning skills because they got into college.

The underlying problem is that, when it comes to learning, we believe the easier, the better. But, harder is better. Robert Bjork, a well-known researcher of adult learning, captured this more than twenty-five years ago in his notion of "desirable difficulties."[8] Introducing some difficulties into the learning process greatly improves long-term retention of the material.

That probably seems counterintuitive. Generally, our theory of mind tells us if you practice until it's easy, you know it better. You've learned. But, that doesn't mean the *process* of learning works best when it's easy. In fact, you learn better and more if you process the material more deeply, and that takes more, rather than less, work.

Students know this, of course, because they know it's better to read the material twice rather than just once; to read and underline not just read; and to study before a test and not just rely on having gone to class. But they also have some false beliefs about learning. Here are some of them:

1. **Taking notes:** Requiring students to take class notes by hand, and not use their laptops, leads to better learning. It results in better test performance and better retention of information months later. Why? Today's students are so good at using keyboards to type in text (or to text out a message to their friends) that it doesn't require much thinking. It's automatic.

But learning takes conscious attention. It's actually better for their learning if students take notes with pen and paper, the old-fashioned way, because that takes more processing and more attention. As a bonus, it puts the laptop away—a device that is all too easy to use to check e-mail, look up what's showing at the movies, or check a game score during class time.

2. **Underlining:** Underlining what you read does take more effort than just reading, but not much. It's fairly mindless processing. Moreover, underlining encourages the impression that you're studying for the test by later going through what you've underlined. But rereading someone else's words is a poor learning strategy.[9]

A better, but harder, thing to do is to put what you've read into your own words: write in margins, paste in Post-it notes with your ideas and questions, ask yourself for explanations. These work because trying to explain requires deeper processing.

3. **Instructors' materials:** You may remember complaining when a teacher wrote on the board with small or hard-to-read handwriting. Although it seems supremely obvious that clear instructional materials would promote better learning, studies show you learn better from print that's harder to read. There are limits of course; illegible print conveys nothing. But if you have to work harder to process legible materials, that increases learning and retention.

Again, the secret is that it requires more attention, even some sensible gap filling, and that promotes deeper processing. Even seemingly trivial difficulties can help. We learn better if the font is a bit blurry (though still legible) or if the material is printed by hand (with its noticeable irregularities) than if it is precise, identical, machine printing.[10]

As a corollary for teachers, all the work you put into producing perfect PowerPoint slides can work against students' learning. While students evaluate this material favorably, it should be used sparingly. Writing and drawing on the board and having students take their own notes from that are better aids to deeper processing. As much as it goes against our intuitions, making learning materials *less* clear and less clearly organized can promote, not hinder, better learning.

4. **Testing:** Students hate pop quizzes, but research shows they work. Frequent tests aid learning. Self-tests—when students cook up and take their own tests—also work. A key influence here (again) is that taking a test requires more thought and deeper processing than reading or listening to information. It takes work. Quizzes throughout the term also induce students to study and prepare step by step, not all at once. That too aids learning.

Students balk at employing most desirable difficulties because they require more effort early on, but that's the point. That's why they work. More effort leads to better processing and to better retention and learning. It is more difficult. Learning how to learn is itself a desirable difficulty.

How to Get Smarter

We are convinced learning takes intelligence—smarts. But, adults and children often misunderstand what that means because they harbor unhelpful, everyday theories of intelligence. Carol Dweck, a psychologist at Stanford University, has spent more than thirty years showing us some of our errors and their power.

Dweck and her students outlined two different everyday theories of intelligence, which she calls mindsets.[11] Many children and adults have a *fixed mindset* (also called an *entity theory*). For them, intelligence is an entity, and different people have different amounts of it. If you're smart, you have a high amount; if you're not so smart, you have less. Your amount of intelligence doesn't change, but it can be revealed or hidden on various tasks, like solving problems, taking tests, and working on projects. Revealing your (fixed) intelligence is what happens when you tackle a test or when you approach learning in an instructional setting, like a classroom, a workshop, or an evaluation.

In contrast, some children and adults have a malleable *growth mindset* (or an *incremental theory* of intelligence). They understand that whatever your

---

Sidebar 13.1. Inspiring a Growth Mindset

Of course, your current ideas can be entrenched and difficult to adjust and reframe. In her book *Mindsets*, Dweck gives some suggestions about how to tackle this.

Both parents and teachers hear a lot about the importance of self-esteem for their children, and often they have been advised to praise their children's intelligence and abilities. Do it often and consistently, this advice says, because that will bolster and boost children's confidence, esteem, and efforts.

But Dweck's research shows this kind of praise often backfires. Praising intelligence creates a fixed mindset and an aversion to challenge. In her research, children were delighted when they received this praise. But, when they hit an obstacle, their belief in their fixed ability convinced them they were not smart enough to tackle it. Their performance plummeted. In contrast are children who are praised for their *process*, such as their hard work or their good strategies. Children who saw these as the reasons for their good performance had a growth mindset and a mastery-oriented reaction to difficulty.

Research shows that even parents and teachers who have a growth mindset themselves can fail to convey this to their children. This is because adults' words and deeds don't line up with their mindsets. Dweck's most recent research has shown that many parents and teachers who endorse a growth mindset fail to use process praise. These same adults also react with concern or anxiety about children's ability when the child fails. A more growth-oriented reaction would be sending the message that difficulty, failure, and confusion are good things. They pave the way for further progress.

initial intelligence, it can always change: It can increase; you can get smarter. With a growth mindset, getting smarter is the goal in problem-solving. Challenges, setbacks, and high effort are important parts of learning; they help you get smarter. When studying children's problem-solving, Dweck was at first surprised when some grade schoolers confronting difficulty said things like, "I love a challenge," "I was *hoping* this would be hard," or "Mistakes are our friend."*

But, for those with fixed mindsets, challenges, setbacks, and even high effort are risky. They can result in a judgment, from others or from themselves, that their fixed intelligence was wanting.

Many, many children and adults have a fixed mindset. But research shows that a growth mindset is more accurate. You *can* learn more (Sidebar 13.1).

Always Working

Theory of mind is at work in ways big and small, in ways hidden and obvious. Societally, it shapes our legal and moral codes, our written and pictorial conventions, and our screen media. Individually, it shapes our feelings, our gift giving, our teaching and learning, or our failures to learn. It's at work in adults and in children and in the way we can bring those parts of ourselves together. It is a foundational piece of who we were, who we are, who we will become, and how those knit together.

* This is a dawning youthful appreciation for some of the advantages of desirable difficulties.

14

Stories, Theories, Minds

Cinderella is a classic story of dignity in the face of oppression, with virtue (and beauty) rewarded in the end. It's more classic than many Americans know. We're most likely to remember the Brothers Grimm story or the 1950s Disney animated film and its derivations. But, the Greeks had the story of *Rhodopis*, a Greek slave girl whose sandal falls in the lap of an Egyptian pharaoh. He sends men across the country to find its wearer. Rhodopis is brought before the pharaoh, enchants him, and they are wed.

Folklorists argue the basic story is nearly universal. There are Chinese versions dating from the 800s and Arabian versions, and hundreds of variations known historically and worldwide. These include films (*Lying to be Perfect, Elle: A Modern Cinderella Tale*); musicals; operas (*Cendrillon, La Cenicienta*); and novels for adults (*Confessions of an Ugly Stepsister*) and for children (*Bella at Midnight*).

Throughout *Reading Minds*, I've used stories—Shakespeare's stories, *People* magazine stories, comic book stories, children's stories—to help illuminate our everyday uses of theory of mind. Stories present our lives and explicate people. The power and appeal of narrative—of stories, of gossip, of dramas that portray human lives and actions—are arguably universal. But that universe is complex.

The story of *Cinderella* rests on Cinderella's roles (stepdaughter, maid) and the roles of others (stepmother, fairy godmother) and on her actions (cleaning and scrubbing, going to the ball). Underlying those, the story depends on Cinderella's wants (to go to the ball) and thoughts (that it's hopeless to think she'll get there), as well as the obstacles (her need to complete her mountain of chores) that shape her actions and emotions as events unfold. *Cinderella* uses concepts like secrets, lies, mysteries, clues, false beliefs, and extraordinary minds that saturate *Reading Minds* and reading minds. Cinderella keeps her identity secret at the ball; the only clue is her discarded slipper. The stepsisters, when trying on the slipper brought by the prince's men, falsely claim it is theirs. A fairy godmother's ideas, plans, and deceptions lace the story together.

Reading Minds. Henry M. Wellman with Karen Lind, Oxford University Press (2020) © Oxford University Press.
DOI: 10.1093/oso/9780190878672.001.0001

That narrative—all narrative—involves situations and actions linked together by *minds*. Characters in fiction, be they simplified archetypes like Cinderella or complex personalities like Elizabeth Bennett, chart complicated paths and spin myriad thoughts. Yet, we understand and identify with them easily. Theory of mind allows us to do so.

Without the underpinning of mind, authors couldn't write fiction and readers couldn't understand it. Authors create credible fictional characters by fabricating for them wants, thoughts, feelings, plans, hopes, preferences, and actions that satisfy or thwart their intentions—all characteristics within the framework of ordinary theory of mind. The characters become believable when their details correspond with our commonly accepted, everyday psychological explanations. This is why stories cannot be completely, purely fictional. They must be based on an everyday psychology that a reader can understand or else there is nothing we can relate to.

Astronomers, such as those at SETI (Search for Extraterrestrial Life Institute), face this problem when searching for signs of life elsewhere in the universe. Here's a thought experiment: Try to think of an extraterrestrial of such alien-ness it doesn't resemble human life in the least. Real aliens could in fact be so alien we'd never recognize them, their signals, their chemistry, or their traces. They could completely escape notice because they would be unfathomable without some anchoring in our ordinary human theories. Contact and communication with such an alien life form could well be impossible. Could you, or anyone, recognize that when you see it? Our malleable, rubber-band–like theory of mind can stretch only so far without breaking apart.

Science fiction writers must cope with this problem. Their extraordinary aliens are, and must be, created within the confines of our ordinary theory of mind. Otherwise, they wouldn't make sense to the author or to the reader. There would be no story. For the same reasons, it's no coincidence that people who report abduction by aliens in UFOs always report the aliens want something (sex, information, resources); have thoughts (even mental telepathy); and engage in deception.

The Stories We Live By

Cinderella is an archetypal story that some people identify as akin to their own life story. They draw parallels between this common, public story and their own, private, life story. A life story is one's autobiography. Arguably, it is bound up with our self-identity: It helps us make sense of both personal consistencies and personal change. The title of Dan McAdams' (1993) book, *The Stories We Live By*, captures the way we structure our lives as narrative.[1]

David Copperfield, acknowledged as the most autobiographical of Charles Dickens' novels, provides an example. To preface the book, Dickens wrote, "Whether I will turn out to be the hero of my own life, or whether that station will be held by anybody else, these pages must show."[2] He exploits his own life story to create fiction. Other great writers exploit others' life stories, as when Sophocles tells us Oedipus's tragic story. Psychologists may then exploit these "fictional" lives: Freud argued that we all live through an Oedipal story in our childhoods. Some stories so accurately capture our everyday understandings they become templates for further understandings.

Lay folk, Dickens, and cognitive scientists call our self-recollections our "autobiographical memories." These memories, which acknowledge the link between narrative, story, and self, emerge in preschool, based in part on still earlier stories about one's deeds and experiences told by parents and kin. In adolescence, life stories get more extended, more coherent, and more story-like, and they become increasingly self-defining. It is often in adolescence that youth try to find a narrative thread for their life. Their story may include lessons learned or misdeeds that corrupted; it may be a story of potency or happenstance, of personal consistency or of personal change; it may feature themselves as hero or victim. Increasingly adolescents and young adults create broad stories for their lives, stories that explain how they have come to be who they are.

An especially American identity narrative is what McAdams calls the *redemptive* story. It's the story of a hero who encounters a dangerous world with steadfastness and courage. He or she overcomes suffering and setbacks and in the end achieves success or well-being. The hero creates not only a positive life course but also a positive impact on others. As McAdams put it, "Americans seem to love redemptive life stories, variations of which include narratives of religious atonement, upward mobility, personal emancipation, and recovery." We see (and learn from) them in the cherished stories of Abraham Lincoln, Rosa Parks, Barak Obama, Eleanor Roosevelt, and *Cinderella*.

Autobiographies, *our* stories, are not a random sequence of events. They portray our minds and the actions our minds generate over the course of our lives. Autobiographies work like all stories, recruiting the power and the resources of theory of mind to characterize an individual, in this case your-self. They include our thoughts, wants, hopes, actions, feelings, and plans. We use our everyday theory of mind to integrate these, allowing us to under-stand ourselves and to create the stories we live by.

Stories are everywhere,[3] and underpinning them is a theory of mind that impacts our ideas about fact and fiction, right and wrong, feelings and thoughts, friends and enemies, learning and failure.

Self-Deceptions and Errors

Human errors are at least as ubiquitous as stories and can be as dependent on theory of mind. If you've read this far, you know our theory of mind works overtime *and* its constructions can't always be trusted. Our life stories can be inflated: trials and tribulations embellished, misdeeds ignored (for a redemp-tive life story) or overweighted (for an atonement life story). Self-narratives can include errors that dupe even ourselves. Our everyday mind reading is prone to mistakes because theories of mind are always *construals*, not facts. We can see this clearly as we try to read emotions.

Understanding and Misunderstanding Emotions

In some sense, we're all experts in emotion. We observe the emotions of others, and we make decisions based on emotions we hope to arouse. We pursue something because we think it will make us happy, or we avoid some-thing because we worry it will anger someone else.

Despite living intimately with emotion, there's a lot we don't know. Sometimes, we're baffled by our own or others' emotional responses. Sometimes, we wish we could change our emotions but don't know how. These, and other, related problems, grow from the constraints of our eve-ryday theories about emotion.

William James is generally considered to be the father of American psy-chology. Born into a highly educated family, he was the brother of Henry James, the famous novelist, and he regularly associated with Ralph Waldo Emerson (his godfather), Mark Twain, Bertrand Russell, Walter Lippmann, and the like. He wrote broadly and insightfully on religion, education, pragmatism, and of course, psychology. He taught Harvard's first course on psychology, and his book, *The Principles of Psychology,* was the ground-breaking text in the field, was immensely influential, and is often cited to this day. He became one of the most influential thinkers of the late nineteenth century.

Principles of Psychology covered many of what are now the standard topics of psychology: thinking, learning, consciousness, instincts, free will, and emotion.[4] James often began by describing the commonsense understanding of a phenomenon and then moved on to craft a deeper interpretation. About emotion, James began, "Common sense says, we lose our fortune, are sorry and weep; we meet a bear, are frightened and run; we are insulted by a rival, are angry and strike."

Situations and objects in the world, what James called "the world's furniture," directly evoke basic emotions like fear, anger, disgust, and joy. Encounter the snake, feel fear; find honey, be happy; be pushed by someone else, feel angry; eat smelly, moldy food, feel disgust turn your stomach. Our commonsense theory of emotion, embedded within our commonsense theory of mind, is a "situationist" theory: Situations—the world's furniture—evoke predictable emotional reactions.

Sometimes, we can train ourselves to overcome these standard emotional reactions—we can learn to fear puppies or happily eat limburger cheese. But, we understand that takes serious learning and enculturation, which acknowledges the power of the initial basic emotional reactions.

More complex emotions like shame and guilt call for more complex processing. Shame is not just basic fear or worry; it's fear or worry that someone else, or our better self, is judging us as transgressing an important standard. Still, the "situationist" view generally holds sway. Emotion scholar Paul Ekman's influential FACS (Facial Action Coding System) was developed to discern and categorize "every facial expression." It is the basis for his claims that people worldwide—in Western, Eastern, and hunter–gatherer cultures—express and recognize a standard set of emotional expressions, such as contentment, excitement, fear, anger, and disgust.[5] It is also the basis of his claims about how to detect deception and lies.

To back up these claims, Ekman used situations he believed would evoke strong emotions everywhere in any culture: the arrival of friends (happiness), something that smells putrid (disgust), or a harmful predator (fear). His expectation of finding these reactions was based on a commonsense situationist theory of emotion.

But, an alternative view insists that emotional experience is much more saturated with theory-of-mind notions than Ekman or James suggested. Call this a "cognitivist" theory of emotion. Cognitive behavioral therapy (CBT) provides a revealing example. CBT can have variations, but in full form it is currently the best evidence-based practice for treating depression and anxiety. It also provides guidelines for better self-understanding.

Aaron Beck is a CBT pioneer, and his theories about treating depression using CBT have been particularly influential.[6] In his view, situations, feelings, behavior, *and thoughts* are always at play in our lives, and they influence one another. Thoughts are a particularly powerful, but often overlooked, influence on even simple feelings like anger and fear. And, they are key in addressing more complex issues like depression, fear of failure, maladaptive coping, anxiety, guilt, and addiction. According to this brand of CBT, it is the interplay of distorted thought and maladaptive behaviors, mediated by feelings, that is responsible for distress, stress, and problematic mental health. Changing maladaptive thinking—that is, false beliefs—will lead to changes in *affect* and behavior. CBT tackles the *cognition* in a cognitivist account of emotions.

One of the key techniques of CBT is to ask clients to bring up their theories of mind and emotion. Then, they're challenged (or they challenge themselves) to reframe and revise the dysfunctional parts of their ideas. For example, some depressives engage in excessive mind reading that yields negative emotional reactions. If they're giving a talk, for instance, they might think their audience is thinking, "What dumb ideas," "Why is he wearing that too-formal (or too-informal) attire?" or "Yawn, so what?" The depressive's resulting negative emotions impair performance and, more chronically, cause depressive symptoms.

In CBT, these people are taught some different ideas:

1. Their mind-reading thoughts are just thoughts, and they might very well be wrong.
2. Their thoughts don't need to provoke emotions (a reframing challenge that can be successful).
3. Emotion doesn't confirm a thought (that's a dysfunctional thought–emotion link that needs to be reframed). If you're feeling anxious as you begin your talk, that doesn't mean you genuinely have something to fear; it's probably just normal, predictable butterflies.

When people have more insight into their emotions and adopt this alternate cognitivist theory of emotion, they can better control their emotions, and they can become less depressed or anxious.

There is history for and scope to this alternative theory of emotion. Ancient stoics believed that logic and awareness should be used to discard false beliefs that produce destructive emotions. Buddhists believe that our deeply felt attractions and repulsions to situations—to the world's furniture—are illusions distorting our worldviews and obscuring a better, and a more serene, way of living and thinking.

It's Magic

Sometimes errors are deliberately triggered. Magicians do it all the time. Magicians are expert at creating striking effects, often without special lighting or quick reflexes. (The claim that magic works because "the hand is quicker than the eye" is not the basis of most magic.) Magicians beguile us by misdirection, by exploiting our habits of mind, and by creating false beliefs[7]—all within the sphere of our everyday theory of mind.

Imagine a man throwing a red ball into the air in plain sight. He throws it once, closing his hand as the ball releases, then opening his hand to catch the ball as it returns. He throws it again, doing exactly what he did the first time. The third time, when he throws, the ball disappears in midair. The man stares at his hand in disbelief and waves his empty hand, looking where the ball should have landed. People gasp.

You swear you saw the ball disappear in midflight, but, of course, the ball can't disappear. How is it done? Misdirection.

The first two times the magician throws the ball, he's training you to see and expect the ball in flight: up and return, up and return. His hand opens, then closes, then opens again to catch the ball. And he moves his eyes up then down following the ball's falling flight. The third time as he tosses his hand up, he keeps his hand shut with the ball inside, but he looks up and down along the path of the ball just as before. While his eyes go down (and yours do, too), he moves the ball surreptitiously to his other hand. Finally, he opens his tossing hand, now waiting the receive the ball like always, but the hand remains empty. Presto! He caps off the trick by staring at his empty hand and waving it in disbelief.

Often, as an epilogue for the trick, after a few astonished seconds, he uses his other hand to reach into midair where the ball should have travelled and pulls the red ball (apparently) right out of thin air. Gasp again.

When I describe it like this, it's hard to believe the trick works. It's so obvious. But that's the power of what is called "mental forcing." The magician forces your mind to expect and see certain things. In fact, even when you know the secret of this trick, a good magician can force the effect so strongly, you see the ball disappear anyway.

For this trick, and for many others, all the action takes place in plain sight at normal speed. That's part of the trick: Audiences don't believe they could fail to see and know something so obvious. This is dictated by our theory-of-mind thinking: Actions in plain sight clearly reveal themselves. But, this is a false belief.

Novice magicians, still in thrall to this theory-of-mind belief, are often tormented with "magician's guilt." They fear spectators will notice immediately how the trick is done. More experienced magicians coach their apprentices not only by providing advice on how to improve their technical skills, but also by reassuring them that their fear of getting caught is largely unwarranted. With increased practice and experience—often in the form of performing plain-sight tricks in public in spite of their guilty fear—novice magicians learn to overcome their natural intuitions.

They also learn not to perform in front of an audience of three-year-olds. Three-year-olds tend to think, "OK. Ho hum." It's only when children begin to understand false beliefs at age four or five years that they gasp and applaud. They understand people can be fooled, even in plain sight. "Hey, I was watching. Where did it go? That's amazing."

We Don't Know What We Don't Know

There's an old North Carolina saying that goes, "It's not what you don't know that gets you, it's what you think you know." This is obviously a saying about false beliefs. But, more generally, it's about knowing and about false ideas about knowing.

Most people think they know a fair bit about many everyday things. How do bicycles work? Why do we have seasons? Why are temperatures higher in summer than winter?

When adults are asked about seasons and summer temperatures, the most common answer is that the sun is closer to the earth in summer. When asked more about this answer, most adults remark, correctly, that the earth's orbit is not circular, it's elliptical. Sometimes we're closer to the sun and sometimes farther away. Indeed, on average, earth is about 93,960,000 miles from the sun. But, sometimes, at "aphelion," we're about 95,000,000 miles away. Sometimes, at "perihelion," we're about 91,000,000 miles away. We get summer when we're closer and winter when we're farther away—it's a common belief.

Hmm? Actually, in the Northern Hemisphere, we're closer to the sun in winter. On January 15, Minneapolis, Minnesota, is as close to the sun as it ever gets, and January is the coldest month of the year in Minneapolis. I know this well because I got my PhD at the University of Minnesota. Nonetheless, each winter in North America we're closer to the sun than at any other time of year; each summer, we're farthest away.

So, the explanation is not that we're farther or closer to the sun in that sense. Instead, the answer is that we're farther or closer to the sun in a different way. The earth is tilted on its axis. When it's winter in Minneapolis, the earth is tilted away from the sun, and it's tilted toward the sun in Santiago where it's summer. For most, even knowledgeable people, their knowledge stops there; closer equals summer, farther equals winter.

But wait, the earth's tilt on its axis is not that great. It's tilted about 23.5 degrees. That tilt makes almost no difference in total distance to the sun. If Minneapolis is 93,000,000 miles from the sun in winter, Santiago is only a tiny fraction closer—a miniscule difference in the 93,000,000 miles that *both* are from the sun.

In fact, it's not distance; it's the angle of light hitting the earth that creates the different seasons. The tilt influences the refraction of sunlight in the earth's atmosphere. The refraction warms things up, like sunlight trapped in a greenhouse in winter. The tilt in the Sothern Hemisphere in its summer means more refracted light rays are trapped so they produce more heat. Conversely, at the same time in Minnesota's winter, the tilt angles the sun's rays to allow more heat to escape.

By now you're probably saying, "OK! OK! Of course, I don't know all this. That's what astronomers are for!" We know it's about the sun's influence on the earth in general, and someone else knows the details—those guys.

That's a huge, underappreciated point.

Our knowledge is not just in our mind, although we commonly think it is: my brain, my mind, my knowledge. Actually, "our" knowledge resides in a community of minds. We don't live merely individually or in a community of bodies; we live in a community of minds. We would not be such competent thinkers if we had to rely on the limited knowledge stored in our own minds. One secret of our success is that we live in community. Figuratively, we never think alone.[8]

This often-overlooked truth makes reading minds all the more crucial. We join minds, we pool knowledge, we communicate. We crowdsource our knowledge and lives, and we do so via theories of minds. We don't often appreciate this; we don't know what we don't know because it's so easily accessible from others. And its easily accessible because theory of mind is doing its job.

Reading Minds

All day, every day, we get into the minds of other people. We observe their words and actions so we can draw conclusions about their thoughts, feelings, hopes, intentions, and goals. We want to, and do, penetrate into their inner *mental* states. Further, we read, interpret, and communicate our own mental states—to explain ourselves to others, to clarify our thoughts for ourselves, and to generate our actions and interactions.

Reading minds inexorably shapes our lives in ways big and small. It starts in childhood and builds from there. All this takes a framework, it takes a theory, a theory of mind.

> We must all eventually adopt a fundamental framework, some reasonably coherent system of causes and effects that will help us make sense not simply of momentous events, but of all the little actions and interactions that constitute our daily lives.[9]

Virtually every dynamic that defines us as social human beings--ideas about fact and fiction; reality and magic; right and wrong; feelings and thoughts; science and myth; friends and enemies; interactions with humans, animals, and now robots--is saturated with our everyday theories of mind.

Acknowledgments

I owe a very large debt to others who helped inspire, write, edit, and publish this book.

My agent Lauren Sharp at Aevitas Creative Management.

My publisher, Oxford University Press, who has published two of my earlier books but who took a risk on this very different type of project. My editor at Oxford, Joan Bossert.

A friend, John Jamison, read my prior academic tome on this topic, *Making Minds*, and wrote an Amazon review where he said, "I look forward to seeing a book by the same author but directed toward non-specialists." He then went on to read drafts of this book, as did my colleagues Paul Harris and Alison Gopnik. Thank you John, Paul, and Alison.

This book could not have been written without Karen Lind, who labored alongside me on this project. She worked on every word of *Reading Minds*, rewriting most with her own writerly expertise honed in her years of writing about medical science as well as works of fiction. She contributed a lovely sense of what clear, approachable writing should look like—and more.

Authors always end by thanking their families. I do, more than I can possibly express: a family of loving parents, a sister, a brother, and many wonderful cousins. And especially, I'd like to thank my closest family: to you Ned, Daniel, Chelsea, Chase, AJ, Emma and Karen. In a wonderful coincidence, Karen Lind not only worked on this book, she has been my wife for more than forty years.

Notes

Preface

1. **Mindreading brain study:** The NBC News post can be found by going to the NBCNews.com website and searching for "scientists try to predict intentions."

Chapter 1

1. **Chilean mine disaster:** The *People* magazine account of the Chilean mine disaster and the dramatic safe return of the miners to the surface can be found in Tresniowski, A., & McNeil, L. (2010). Chilean mine drama: Hope & survival. *People, 74,* 97–107.
2. **Evolutionary theorizing about theory of mind:** For a 2015 best-selling example, see Yuval Noah Harari's *Sapiens: A brief history of mankind.* New York, NY: Harper.
3. **Bags of skin:** The quotation regarding bags of skin comes from Gopnik, A., Meltzoff, A. N., & Kuhl, P. K. (2001). *The scientist in the crib* (pp. 4–5). New York, NY: HarperCollins.
4. **Parent–child conversations about people and minds:** Most of the quotations from parent–child conversations here and in further chapters (except for those from my sons) come from my 1995 book with Karen Bartsch: *Children talk about the mind.* New York, NY: Oxford University Press.
5. **Mindblind:** This is a phrase first coined by Simon Baron-Cohen for his 1995 book on autism, *Mindblindness.* Cambridge, MA: MIT Press.
6. **Temple Grandin:** Oliver Sacks on Temple Grandin in 1996: *An anthropologist on Mars: Seven paradoxical tales.* New York, NY: Vintage Books. Temple Grandin has a brief biography at her website: http://www.grandin.com/temple.html. She also has two autobiographies: *Emergence: Labeled autistic.* Novato, CA: Arena Press, 1986. and *Thinking in pictures: My life with autism.* New York, NY: Vintage Books, 1995.
7. **Uta Frith:** See her 1989 book, *Autism: Explaining the enigma.* Hoboken, NJ: Blackwell.

Chapter 2

1. **Gossip:** See Dunbar, R., *Grooming, gossip, and the evolution of language.* (1996). London, England: Faber & Faber.
2. **Temple Grandin:** Oliver Sacks's 1996 report on Temple Grandin is in his *An anthropologist on Mars: Seven paradoxical tales.* New York, NY: Vintage Books.
3. *People* **magazine:** The Eva Longoria quotation comes from *People*, February 22, 2016, p. 36. (Emphasis added.)
4. **Colin Powell:** A good source on Colin Powell, his life generally, and his involvement in justifying the Second Gulf War more specifically, can be found in a 2006 book by Karen DeYoung: *Soldier: The life of Colin Powell.* New York, NY: Knopf. For Powell's life in his own words, see 2012's *It worked for me: In life and leadership*, by Colin Powell with Tony Koltz. New York, NY: HarperCollins.
5. **Lies:** For the meta-analyses on lie detecting, see Bond, C., & DePaulo, B. (2006). Accuracy of deception judgments. *Personality and Social Psychology Review, 10*, 214–234. For a review article, see Hartwig, M., & Bond, C. F. (2011). Why do lie-catchers fail? *Psychological Bulletin, 134*, 477–492; the quotation mentioning the global consensus on liars' behaviors comes from page 644 of that article.
6. **More lies:** To read about Ekman's work according to Ekman himself, see his 2001 book, *Telling lies* (New York, NY: Norton). Be sure to get the 2001 third edition; it contains several updates presented in additional chapters not available in the 1985 first edition. The quotation from the student nurses comes from page 55 of that book. The quotation from Tom Brokaw is from pages 90–91 of the same book.
7. **Social intelligence, social brains:** The social intelligence hypothesis as put forth by Nicholas Humphrey is in his 1984 book, *Consciousness regained.* New York, NY: Oxford University Press. The related social brain hypothesis was put forth in 1998 by Robin Dunbar in The social brain hypothesis, *Evolutionary Anthropology: Issues, News, and Reviews, 6*, 178–190.

Chapter 3

1. **Ruby Bridges:** Ruby Bridges spoke in her own words in 1999 about her experiences in the New Orleans school desegregation crisis in her *Through My Eyes.* New York, NY: Barnes & Noble, 1999. John Steinbeck talked in 1962 about his in *Travels with Charley: In search of America.* New York, NY: Viking Press.
2. **Friendlessness:** One compelling study on the nature and effects of friendlessness is Fink, E., Beeger, S., Peterson, C., Slaughter, V., & de Rosnay, M. (2015). Friendlessness and theory of mind. *British Journal of Developmental Psychology, 33*, 1–17. The quotation on the many negative consequences of being friendless comes from that article.
3. **Social relations, friends:** The meta-analysis on peer acceptance and popularity is Slaughter, V., Imuta, K., Peterson, C., & Henry, J. (2015). Meta-analysis of theory of mind and peer popularity in the preschool and early school years. *Child Development, 86*, 1159–1174.

4. **Baka:** The research on theory-of-mind development in the Baka comes from Avis, J., & Harris, P. (1991). Belief-desire reasoning among Baka children: Evidence for a universal conception of mind. *Child Development, 62,* 460–467.

5. **False-belief research:** The meta-analyses summarized here and in Sidebar 3.1 are in Wellman, H., Cross, D., & Watson, J. (2001). A meta-analysis of theory-of-mind development: The truth about false belief. *Child Development, 72,* 655–684; and Liu, D., Wellman, H., Tardif, T., & Sabbagh, M. (2008). Theory of mind development in Chinese children: A meta-analysis of false-belief understanding across cultures and languages. *Developmental Psychology, 44,* 523. For further information on children's developing understanding of false beliefs, see Wellman, H. (2016). *Making Minds.* New York, NY: Oxford University Press,Chapter 3.

6. **Lies research:** A short overview from 2013 of Kang Lee's many studies on lying can be found in his Little liars. *Child Development Perspectives, 7,* 91–96. For further information on children's developing understanding of and use of lying, see Wellman's *Making Minds,* Chapter 3.

7. **Secrets:** The research on secret keeping by Joan Peskin and Vittoria Ardino is their 2003 article, Representing the mental world in children's social behavior: Playing hide and seek and keeping secrets. *Social Development, 12,* 496–512.

8. **Persuasion:** Karen Bartsch has several studies on persuasion. Her first study relating persuasion to children's false-belief understanding was Bartsch, K., London, K., & Campbell, M. D. (2007). Children's attention to beliefs in interactive persuasion tasks. *Developmental Psychology, 43,* 111–120. Virginia Slaughter and her colleagues at the University of Queensland in Australia showed something very similar that had still greater real-life impact. In their study, three- to eight-year-olds had to persuade a resistant puppet to eat raw broccoli or to brush his teeth when the puppet resisted—both common persuasion issues for preschool children. The number and quality of persuasive arguments that children advanced were substantially correlated with success on theory-of-mind tests. This kind of persuasion obviously requires language competence as well. But theory of mind remained a significant predictor of persuasion even when verbal language competence was controlled. See Slaughter, V., Peterson, C., & Moore, C. (2013). I can talk you into it: Theory of mind and persuasion behavior in young children. *Developmental Psychology, 49,* 227.

9. **Meta-analysis on theory of mind and friendship**: See Note 3.

10. **Friendlessnes:** See Note 2.

Chapter 4

1. **Margaret Svendson's early work on imaginary companions:** Svendson, M. (1934). Children's imaginary companions. *Archives of Neurology and Psychiatry, 2,* 985–999.

2. **Contemporary work on imaginary companions:** Marjorie Taylor's 1999 book is full of readable information and research on imaginary companions: *Imaginary companions and the children who create them* (New York, NY: Oxford University Press). Paul Harris

provided an easy-to-read overview of children's understanding of pretense and imagination in 2000 in *The work of the imagination*. Hoboken, NJ: Blackwell.

3. **Piaget as reformer:** One of my favorite Piaget anecdotes, and an example of Piaget's push for reform in our accepted ideas about children, came when he was appointed head of the J. J. Rousseau Institute at the University of Geneva. He promptly changed the institute's logo from a silhouette of an adult leading a child to one of a child leading an adult.

4. **Piaget's work on children's understanding and misunderstanding of mental entities:** See Piaget, J. (1967). *The child's conception of the world*. London, England: Routledge & Keegan Paul. (Original French work published 1929.)

5. **Contemporary research on children's understanding of mental entities:** See Wellman, D., & Estes, D. (1986). Early understanding of mental entities: A reexamination of childhood realism. *Child Development, 57*, 910–923; Estes Wellman, D. H., & Woolley, J. (1989). Children's understanding of mental phenomena. In H. Reese (Ed.), *Advances in child development and behavior* (Vol. *21*, pp. 41–87). New York, NY: Academic Press; and Watson, J., Gelman, S., & Wellman, H. (1998). Young children's understanding of the non-physical nature of thoughts and the physical nature of the brain. *British Journal of Developmental Psychology, 16*, 321–335.

6. **Benjamin Spock:** First titled *The Commonsense Book of Baby and Child* Care in 1948, the fourth edition in 1976 was simply *Baby and Child Care*. New York, NY: Pocket Books.

7. **Overview of research on the broader topic of children's discrimination of fantasy from reality:** Woolley, J. (1997). Thinking about fantasy: Are children fundamentally different thinkers? *Child Development, 68*, 991–1011.

8. **Enid Blyton quotation:** Is from page 149 in Taylor, Imaginary companions.

9. *Pride and Prejudice,* **then and now:** Jane Austen's *Pride and Prejudice* was originally published in 1812 by Egerton. Chapman's 1923 edition has become the standard modern edition. Austen's "advice": Caldwell, K. (2013). *How to speak like Jane Austen and live like Elizabeth Bennet*. Block Island, RI: Island Bound Press.

Chapter 5

1. **Deep Blue:** IBM's description of Deep Blue's artificial intelligence and its chess championship can be found at http://www-03.ibm.com/ibm/history/ibm100/us/en/icons/deepblue/.

2. **Deep learning:** The current big frontier for artificial intelligence is "machine learning" and most recently "deep learning." Machine learning goes beyond Deep Blue. These computer programs not only execute numerous, very fast correlations, the programs learn. Machine learning is what operates IBM's Watson. Watson is the program that has competed on *Jeopardy* several times, often beating the best prior human *Jeopardy* champions. Watson was not pre-programmed with all the world's possible knowledge and trivia. It was programmed to do statistical learning, then let loose

on encyclopedias, tabloid newspapers, and Trivial Pursuit questions and answers. It played *Jeopardy* first against its programmers, then against other humans, learning more and more facts and trivia all the while. It is still learning. But Watson's statistical learning is still not theory learning. It is not based on meanings and explanations and theory–data interactions. Watson's statistical learning is based on amassing (on its own, admittedly) ever-increasing stores of correlations between questions and answers. That is not how we operate and learn using our everyday theories or how scientific theories operate and are revised.

3. **Temple Grandin, thinking in pictures:** In 1995, Grandin described her sense of how she thinks in *Thinking in pictures: My life with autism*. New York, NY: Vintage Books. Her descriptions to Oliver Sacks appear in 1996 in his *An anthropologist on Mars: Seven paradoxical tales*. New York, NY: Vintage Books.

4. **Science is simple:** Hawking presents a reader-friendly version of his views on physics and life in Hawking, S. (1988). *A brief history of time*. New York, NY: Bantam Books, 1988. You can find lists of many quotations from him by searching for Hawking quotes on Google.

5. **Theory or not? Big babies or little scientists?** For further discussion of why young children are not little scientists but are building theories and adult scientists are following in their footsteps, see Chapter 12 of Wellman, H. (2014). *Making minds*. New York, NY: Oxford University Press. For an extended argument on science (and scientific theorizing) as a bad metaphor for child knowledge, see page 206 of Harris, P. (2012). *Trusting what you're told*. Cambridge, MA: Harvard University Press.

Chapter 6

1. **How hearing parents interact with their deaf young children:** Marc Marschark, an expert on deaf children, described interactions between hearing parents and their deaf children in Vaccari, C., & Marschark, M. (1997). Communication between parents and deaf children: Implications for social-emotional development. *Journal of Child Psychology and Psychiatry, 38*, 793–801. For a more readable and comprehensive treatment of his ideas, see Marschark, M. (2007). *Raising and educating a deaf child*. New York, NY: Oxford University Press.

2. **Broccoli versus goldfish studies:** See Repacholi, B. M., & Gopnik, A. (1997). Early reasoning about desires: Evidence from 14- and 18-month-olds. *Developmental Psychology, 33*, 12–21. You can see a clip of Alison Gopnik demonstrating the goldfish and broccoli study on YouTube (https://www.youtube.com/watch?v=GkYQg0l5bMY).

3. **Theory of mind scaling research:** A good overview of the now-considerable research with children—in different countries and for hearing and deaf children—is in Wellman, H. M. (2014). *Making minds*. New York, NY: Oxford University Press, pp. 93–107.

4. **Nicaraguan sign language research:** A good short description of how Nicaraguan Sign Language was created and changed over cohorts is in Senghas, A., Kita, S., &

Ozyürek, A. (2004). Children creating core properties of language: Evidence from an emerging sign language in Nicaragua. *Science, 305*, 1779–1782. A short report of how that influences theory-of-mind understandings is Pyers, J. E., & Senghas, A. (2009). Language promotes false-belief understanding: Evidence from learners of a new sign language. *Psychological Science, 20*, 805–812.

5. **Enhancing theory of mind:** Our research demonstrating that having children provide explanations for false-belief–driven actions enhances their false-belief understandings appears in Amsterlaw, J., & Wellman, H. M. (2006). Theories of mind in transition: A microgenetic study of the development of false belief understanding. *Journal of Cognition and Development, 7*, 139–172.; and Rhodes, M., & Wellman, H. M. (2006). Constructing a new theory from old ideas and new evidence. *Cognitive Science, 37*, 592–604.

6. **China and also Iran:** Despite profound differences between Iran's Muslim traditions and beliefs and Chinese Confucian/Communist ones, both China and Iran share collectivist family values emphasizing consensual learning, knowledge acquisition, and low tolerance for childhood assertions of disagreement or independent belief. Those factors help account for their similar sequences of early theory-of-mind understanding and their differences from children growing up in western-individualistic countries like the United States and Australia.

Chapter 7

1. **Piaget's diaries:** Diary records of Piaget's three children are reported in his three seminal books originally published in the 1920s: *The origins of intelligence.* New York, NY: International Universities Press, 1952; *The construction of reality in the child.* New York, NY: Basic Books, 1954; and *Play, dreams, and imitation in childhood.* New York, NY: Norton, 1962.

2. **Robert Fantz:** See his 1961 work, The origin of form perception. *Scientific American, 204*, 66–72.

3. **Very young infants prefer mom's voice:** Even 2- and 3-day-old newborns prefer to listen to (and will work harder to listen to) their mother's voice (measured by how they suck on pacifiers that record their sucking rates). The classic demonstration comes from DeCasper, A., & Fifer, W.(1980). Of human bonding: Newborns prefer their mothers' voices. *Science, 208*, 1174–1176.

4. **Spelke baby research:** For a good description of Spelke's infant laboratory and her influence on the field, see Talbot, M. (2006). The baby lab: How Elizabeth Spelke peers into the infant mind. *The New Yorker,* September 4.

5. **Woodward's work:** Amanda Woodward began her systematic infant research in 1998 with Infants selectively encode the goal object of an actor. *Cognition, 69*, 1–34. A 2013 readable synopsis of her research program is Infant foundations of intentional understanding. In M. Banaji & S. Gelman (Eds.), Navigating the social world (pp. 75–80). New York, NY: Oxford University Press.

6. **Boxes of ducks and frogs:** For the research with ten-month-olds, see Wellman, H. M., Kushnir, T., Xu, F., & Brink, K. (2016). Infants use statistical sampling to understand the psychological world. *Infancy, 21,* 668–676. For the studies with toddlers, see Kushnir, T., Xu, F., & Wellman, H. M. (2010). Young children use statistical sampling to infer the preferences of others. *Psychological Science, 21,* 1134–1140.

7. **Infants understand false beliefs?** The Onishi and Baillargeon study (the first on infant false-belief understanding) is Onishi, R., & Baillargeon, R. (2005). Do 15-month-old infants understand false beliefs? *Science, 308,* 255–258. In reviewing all the contemporary research, Hannes Rackoczy has shown that results are mixed, and many infant false-belief studies did not replicate the original research. (Repeats of the study showed no significant effect.) See Kulke, H., & Rakoczy, H. (2018). Implicit theory of mind—An overview of current replications and non-replications. *Data in Brief,* 16, 101–104. A good example of such research is Dorrenberg, S., Rackoczy, H., & Liszkowski, U. (2018). How (not) to measure infant theory of mind: Testing the replicability and validity of four non-verbal measures. *Cognitive Development, 46,* 12–30.

8. **Deaf infants of hearing parents:** The research showing that deaf infants of hearing parents do not show an understanding of false belief when tested with standard infant looking-time methods is by Meristo, M., Morgan, G., Geraci, A., Iozzi, L., Hjelmquist, E., Surian, L., & Siegal, M. (2012). Belief attribution in deaf and hearing infants. *Developmental Science, 15,* 633–640.

9. **Elizabeth Spelke quotes:** On infant core innate capacities, see Spelke, E., & Kinzler, K. (2009). Innateness, learning, and rationality. *Child Development Perspectives, 3,* 96–98. For the Spelke infants "enagage with people," see Angier, N. (2012). From the minds of babes. *New York Times,* May 1.

Chapter 8

1. **OMG:** See Parker, M. (2016). *OMG, How children see God.* Deerfield Beach, FL: Health Communications.

2. **Other child quotes:** These come mostly from Barbour, M., & Barbour, B. (2001). *What kids say about life, love, and God.* Ulrichsville, OH: Promise Press.

3. **Barrett study and preparedness:** Barrett, J., Richert, R., & Driesenga, A. (2001). God's beliefs versus mother's: The development of nonhuman agent concepts. *Child Development, 72,* 50–65. For writing of Barrett's on preparedness, see Barrett, J., & Richert, R. (2003). Anthropomorphism or preparedness? Exploring children's God concepts. *Review of Religious Research, 44,* 300–312. For an easy to read account of Barrett's ideas and interpretations read Barrett, J. (2012) *Born believers: The science of children's religious belief.* Free Press, New York NY.

4. **Our research on children's, at first quite limited, early steps in understanding of extraordinary minds:** Lane, J., Wellman, H., & Evans, E. (2010). Children's understanding of ordinary and extraordinary minds. *Child Development, 81,* 1475–1489.

Lane, J., Wellman, H., & Evans, M. (2012). Sociocultural input facilitates children's developing understanding of extraordinary minds. *Child Development, 83*, 1007–1021.

5. **Pew Research Center polling of religion in America:** Pew Forum on Religion & Public Life. (2008). U.S. Religious Landscape survey. Religious beliefs and practices: Diverse and politically relevant. Retrieved from http://www.pewforum.org/.

6. **Cognitive science of religion:** Scientific study of the nature of people's belief in religion and religious ideas took on new life in the 1990s in research by cognitive scientists, anthropologists, and religious scholars under the heading of the "cognitive science of religion." For a brief insightful review, see Barrett, J. (2000). Exploring the natural foundations of religion. *Trends in Cognitive Sciences, 4*, 29–34. For an early book-length treatment, see Boyer, P. (1994). *The naturalness of religious ideas: A cognitive theory of religion.* Berkeley, CA: University of California Press. Also see McCauley, R., & Whitehouse, H. (2005). Introduction: New frontiers in the cognitive science of religion. *Journal of Cognition and Culture, 5*, 1–13.

7. **Theological views on omniscience:** Packer, J. I. (1993). *Concise theology: A guide to historic Christian beliefs.* Carol Stream, IL: Tyndale House. Also Surah Al-Mujadila: Qur'an, 58:7.

8. **Robert Coles:** The various quotations from Coles throughout the chapter come from his more than thirty years of listening to children and in this 1990 case: *The spiritual life of children.* Boston, MA: Houghton Mifflin.

9. A special thank you to Chad Thornton at Stadium Cards and Comics in Ypsilanti, Michigan, for generously sharing his vast knowledge of superheroes and superheroines.

10. **Our research on children's understanding of omniscience:** Lane, J., Wellman, H., & Evans, M. (2014). Approaching an understanding of omniscience from the preschool years to early adulthood. *Developmental Psychology, 50*, 2380–2392.

11. **Adults have trouble with omniscience:** Barrett, J., & Keil, F. (1996). Conceptualizing a non-natural entity: Anthropomorphism in God concepts. *Cognitive Psychology, 31*, 219–247.

12. **Carl Johnson quotation:** This is from Johnson's The meaning of death: What my young daughter taught me. Published in 2019 in *UU World: Magazine of the Unitarian Universalist Association.*

13. **Research on children's understanding of death and afterlife:** Harris, P., & Giménez, M. (2005). Children's acceptance of conflicting testimony: The case of death. *Journal of Cognition and Culture, 5*, 143–164. Giménez-Dasí, M., Guerrero, S., & Harris, P. (2005). Intimations of immortality and omniscience in early childhood. *European Journal of Developmental Psychology, 2*, 285–297. Lane, J., Zhu, L., Evans, M., & Wellman, H. (2016). Developing concepts of the mind, body, and afterlife: Exploring the roles of narrative context and culture. *Journal of Cognition and Culture, 15*, 50–82.

14. **Children's understanding (and misunderstanding) of the brain and mind:** Johnson, C., & Wellman, H. (1982). Children's developing conceptions of the mind and brain. *Child Development, 53*, 222–234.

15. **Soul:** Richert, R., & Harris, P. (2006). The ghost in my body: Children's developing concept of the soul. *Journal of Cognition and Culture, 6*, 409–427.

16. **Carl Johnson's research on brain transplants:** Johnson, C. (1990). If you had my brain, where would I be? Children's understanding of the brain and identity. *Child Development, 61,* 962–972. Since this initial study, others have confirmed and extended Johnson's basic results.

Chapter 9

1. **The Baining:** See Fajans, J. (1985). The person in social context: The social character of Baining "Psychology." In G. White & J. Kirkpatrick (Eds.), *Person, self, and experience: Exploring pacific ethnopsychologies* (pp. 367–397). Berkeley, CA: University of California Press.
2. **When God Talks Back:** See Luhrmann, T. (2012). *When God talks back: Understanding the American evangelical relationship with God.* New York, NY: Knopf.
3. Mahayana **Buddhism:** See Williams, P. (with A. Tribe). (2000). *Buddhist thought: A complete introduction to the Indian tradition.* Abingdon, England: Routledge. The other main arm of Buddhism is Therevada, also covered by Williams. There are also Zen Buddhism and other varieties.
4. **Other strikingly different folk psychologies:** For a shortish, older review, see Lillard, A. (1998). Ethnopsychologies: Cultural variations in theories of mind. *Psychological Bulletin, 123,* 3–32. For a longer, more contemporary treatment, compiled by anthropologists studying different cultural groups, see Lurhmann and multiple other authors who contributed to the entire 2011, Volume 36, fourth issue of Toward an anthropological theory of mind in *Suomen Anthropolgi: Journal of the Finnish Anthropological Society.*
5. **Contradictions:** From Whitehead, A. N. (1925). Religion and science. *The Atlantic,* August.
6. **Ideal emotions:** In Chinese versus U.S. adults: Tsai, J. (2007). Ideal affect: Cultural causes and behavioral consequences. *Perspectives on Psychological Science, 2,* 242–259. In Chinese and U.S. children: Tsai, J. L., Louie, J. Y., Chen, E. E., & Uchida, Y. (2007). Learning what feelings to desire: Socialization of ideal affect through children's storybooks. *Personality and Social Psychology Bulletin, 33,* 17–30.

Chapter 10

1. **Jane Goodall:** Goodall has appeared in many TV film documentaries, including the BBC one I mention here. Her seminal book was Goodall, J. (1971). *In the shadow of man.* New York, NY: Collins.
2. **Chimp "language":** A nice treatment of the early chimp language studies, including the research on Washoe by the Gardners, and then the step-by-step dismantling of the "rich" accounts, is provided in Hoff, E. (2009). *Language development.* Belmont, CA: Wadsworth.

3. **Daniel Povinelli:** A thorough reporting of Povinelli's research on chimpanzee's misunderstanding of seeing is in Povinelli, D., & Eddy, T. (1996). What young chimpanzees know about seeing. *Monographs of the Society for Research in Child Development, 61*, entire Serial No. 24). A shorter overview can be found in Povinelli, D., & Preuss, T. (1995). Theory of mind: Evolutionary history of a cognitive specialization. *Trends in Neurosciences, 18*, 418 and following.

4. **Michael Tomasello's early lean interpretations:** The "definitive" treatise on non-human primate cognition as based on research up through the 1990s is Tomasello, M., & Call, J., (1997). *Primate cognition.* New York, NY: Oxford University Press.

5. **Tomasello's later research supporting much richer interpretations:** The first summary of the newer research, still very readable, clear, and short, is Tomasello, M., Call, J., & Hare, B. (2003). Chimpanzees understand psychological states—the question is which ones and to what extent. *Trends in Cognitive Sciences, 7*, 153–156. A more thorough (but still short and readable) treatment appeared in Call, J., & Tomasello, M. (2008). Does the chimpanzee have a theory of mind? 30 years later. *Trends in Cognitive Sciences, 12*, 187–192. A revised update of the earlier views in the 1997 *Primate Cognition* book appears in Seed, A., & Tomasello, M. (2010). Primate cognition. *Topics in Cognitive Science, 2*, 407–419.

6. **Young children spontaneously help others (chimps, not so much):** A good, readable treatment of the research on helping, with both children and apes, is Warneken, F., & Tomasello, M. (2009). Varieties of altruism in children and chimpanzees. *Trends in Cognitive Sciences, 13*, 397–402. The quotation from Felix Warneken comes from that article.

7. **Infants like and aid helpers, not hinderers:** Hamlin, J. K. (2013). Moral judgment and action in preverbal infants and toddlers: Evidence for an innate moral core. *Current Directions in Psychological Science, 22*(3), 186–193

8. **Dogs and domesticated foxes:** A readable summary of the research on theory of mind in dogs and its relation to canine temperament (the "social–emotional reactivity" hypothesis) is Hare, B., & Tomasello, M. (2005). Human-like social skills in dogs? *Trends in Cognitive Sciences, 9*, 439–444. Brian Hare talked about his research on dogs in *The Genius of Dogs* (2013) A Plume Book, New York NY. A recent, readable "memoir" of the Siberian fox studies is Dugatkin, L., & Trut, L. (2017). *How to tame a fox (and build a dog).* Chicago, IL: University of Chicago Press.

9. **Timmy's in the well:** Many dog owners also believe their dogs would help save them from danger (run to go get help) as Lassie did for Timmy in a famous TV show. Probably not, as recent research showed: Macpherson, K., & Roberts, W. (2006). Do dogs (*Canis familiaris*) seek help in an emergency? *Journal of Comparative Psychology, 120*, 113–119.

10. **Temperament and theory-of-mind development in children:** Our first study on this (with three-year-olds who were later tested as 5-year-olds) was Wellman, H., Lane, J., Labounty, J., & Olson, S. (2011). Observant, nonaggressive temperament predicts theory of mind development. *Developmental Science, 14*, 319–326. The follow-up study with U.S. and Chinese children is Lane, J., Wellman, H., Olson, S., Miller, A., Wang, L., & Tardif, T. (2013). Relations between temperament and theory of mind

development in the United States and China: Biological and behavioral correlates of preschoolers' false-belief understanding. *Developmental Psychology, 49,* 825–836.

11. **Social intelligence and the social brain:** See Humphrey, N. (1984). *Consciousness regained: Chapters in the development of mind.* New York, NY: Oxford University Press, 1984. Robin Dunbar overviewed the related social brain hypothesis and the cross-species data on brain size and intelligence in Dunbar, R. (1998). The social brain hypothesis. *Evolutionary Anthropology: Issues, News, and Reviews, 6,* 178–190. His quotation on learning social cognition is from Dunbar, R. (2013). An evolutionary basis for social cognition. In M. Legerstee, D. Haley, & M. Bornstein (Eds.), *The infant mind: Origins of the social brain* (pp. 3–18). New York, NY: Guilford Press.

12. **Child–primate parallels in understanding other's intention:** For children, Behne, T., Carpenter, M., Call, J., & Tomasello, M. (2005). Unwilling versus unable: Infants' understanding of intentional action. *Developmental Psychology, 41,* 328–337. For chimpanzees, Call, J., Hare, B., Carpenter, M., & Tomasello, M. (2004). "Unwilling" versus "unable": Chimpanzees' understanding of human intentional action. *Developmental Science, 7,* 488–498, 2004.

Chapter 11

1. **Cells that read minds:** See Blakeslee, S. (2006, January 10). Cells that read minds. *New York Times.* Retrieved from http://search.proquest.com.proxy.lib.umich.edu/docview/433260430?accountid=14667

2. **Direct recording from neurons in humans:** See Mukamel, R., Ekstrom, A. D., Kaplan, J., Iacoboni, M., & Fried, I. (2010). Single-neuron responses in humans during execution and observation of actions. *Current Biology, 20,* 750–756.

3. **Analysis and review of research on human mirror system:** Van Overwalle, F., & Baetens, K. (2009). Understanding others' actions and goals by mirror and mentalizing systems: A meta-analysis. *NeuroImage, 48,* 564–584.

4. **Lack of automatic imitation and cataracts:** See McKyton, A., Ben-Zion, I., & Zohary, T. (2018). Lack of automatic imitation in newly sighted individuals. *Psychological Science, 29,* 304–310.

5. **Contagious yawning:** In infants: Anderson, J. R., & Meno, P. (2003). Psychological influences on yawning in children. *Current Psychology Letters, 11.* Retrieved from http://cpl.revues.org/document390.html. In dogs: Romero, T., Konno, A., & Hasegawa, T. (2013). Familiarity bias and physiological responses in contagious yawning by dogs support link to empathy. *PLoS One, 8*(8). http://dx.doi.org/10.1371/journal.pone.0071365

6. **Theory-of-mind network:** Described in Carrington, S., & Bailey, A. (2009). Are there theory of mind regions in the brain? A review of the neuroimaging literature. *Human Brain Mapping, 30,* 2313–2335.

7. **Adult brain activations for theory of mind:** Inferring mind from the eyes via fMRI: Baron-Cohen, S., Ring, H., Wheelwright, S., Bullmore, E., Brammer, M.,

Simmons, A., & Williams, S. (1999). Social intelligence in the normal and autistic brain: An fMRI study. *European Journal of Neuroscience, 11*, 1891–1898. And from ERP: Sabbagh, M., Moulson, M. & Harkness, K. (2004). Neural correlates of mental state decoding in human adults: An event-related potential study. *Journal of Cognitive Neuroscience, 16*, 415–426.

8. **Adult brain activations for inferring beliefs**: Via fMRI: Sommer, M., Döhnel, K., Sodian, B., Meinhardt, J., Thoermer, C., & Hajak, G. (2007). Neural correlates of true and false belief reasoning. *NeuroImage, 35*, 1378–1384. Saxe, R., & Wexler, A. (2005). Making sense of another mind: The role of the right temporo-parietal junction. *Neuropsychologia, 43*, 1391–1399. Via ERP: Liu, D., Sabbagh, M., Gehring, W., & Wellman, H. (2004). Decoupling beliefs from reality in the brain: An ERP study of theory of mind. *NeuroReport, 15*, 991–995.

9. **Neurocognitive processing in children**: A good recent description of the child research, summarized in terms of these three points, appears in Wellman, H. (2018). Theory of mind: The state of the art. *European Journal of Developmental Psychology, 15*, 728–755. doi:10.1080/17405629.2018.1435413. A shorter, less technical summary is in Wellman, H. (2017). The development of theory of mind: Historical reflections. *Child Development Perspectives, 11*, 207–214.

Chapter 12

1. *I, Robot*: Isaac Asimov's robot short stories were originally published in science fiction magazines in the 1940s. Then, they were collected into Asimov, I. (1950). *I, Robot*. New York, NY: Gnome Press.

2. **Report on the future of robots in human life**: The National Robotics Initiative is a National Science Foundation program to fund research designed to "accelerate the development and use of robots that work beside or cooperatively with people." Its initiating document was "The National Robotics Initiative 2.0: Ubiquitous Collaborative Robots (NRI-2.0)," (2017).

3. **The uncanny valley**: Adult roboticists first posited the uncanny valley, the surge in feelings of creepiness if robots start to appear and act too human-like. See MacDorman, K. & Ishiguro, H. (2006). The uncanny advantage of using androids in cognitive and social science research. *Interaction Studies, 7*, 297–337. Psychologists then confirmed its presence with adult participants, see Gray, K., & Wegner, D. M. (2012). Feeling robots and human zombies: Mind perception and the uncanny valley. *Cognition, 125*, 125–130.

4. **Uncanny valley feelings develop in childhood**: See Kimberly Brink, K., Gray, K., & Wellman, H. (2019). Creepiness creeps in: Uncanny valley feelings are acquired in childhood. *Child Development, 90*, 1202–1214. doi:10.1111/cdev.12999

5. **Children learn from robots**: Our research: Brink, K., & Wellman, H. Robot teachers for children? Young children trust robots depending on their perceived accuracy and agency. Manuscript submitted for publication.

6. **Research shows that young children are more likely to learn from human-like robots than older children:** The table-setting task: Okita, S. Y., Ng-Thow-Hing, V., & Sarvadevabhatla, R. (2009). Learning together: ASIMO developing an interactive learning partnership with children. Paper presented at the Robot and Human Interactive Communication, RO-MAN 2009 18th IEEE International Symposium. Robovie interacts with children at school: Kanda, T., Hirano, T., Eaton, D., & Ishiguro, H. (2004). Interactive robots as social partners and peer tutors for children: A field trial. *Human-Computer Interaction, 19,* 61–84.

7. **Morality and aggression against robots:** The hitchhiking robot that was vandalized: Victor, D. (2015, August 3). Hitchhiking robot, safe in several countries, meets its end in Philadelphia. *The New York Times.* Children abusing robots: Nomura, T., Kanda, T., Kidokoro, H., Suehiro, Y., & Yamada, S. (2017). Why do children abuse robots? *Interaction Studies, 17,* 347–369.

8. **How to robot-proof your child:** Williams, A. (2017, December 11). Will robots take our children's jobs? *New York Times.*

9. **Morality and prosocial actions toward robots:** Preschool children comfort and protect a robot: Carey, B., & Markoff, J. (2010, July 10). Students, meet your new teacher, Mr. Robot. *The New York Times.* Retrieved from http://nyti.ms/1H9yiEN. Children claim that a robot deserves to be treated fairly and not harmed: Kahn, P. H., Kanda, T., Ishiguro, H., Freier, N. G., Severson, R. L., Gill, B. T., Shen, S. (2012). "Robovie, you'll have to go into the closet now": Children's social and moral relationships with a humanoid robot. *Developmental Psychology, 48,* 303–314.

Chapter 13

1. **In Cold Blood:** Capote, T. (1996). *In cold blood: A true account of a multiple murder and its consequences.* New York, NY: Random House.

2. **Model Penal Code:** See the information on the Model Penal Code provided by the American Law Institute at https://www.ali.org/publications/show/model-penal-code/.

3. **Children and thought bubbles:** Dyer, J. R., Shatz, M. & Wellman, H. M. (2000). Young children's storybooks as a source of mental state information. *Cognitive Development, 15,* 17–37. Wellman, H. M., Hollander, M. & Schult, C. A. (1996). Young children's understanding of thought-bubbles and of thoughts. *Child Development, 67,* 768–788.

4. **Children prefer to explain the unexpected:** See Legare, C., Gelman, S., & Wellman, H. (2010). Inconsistency with prior knowledge triggers children's causal explanatory reasoning. *Child Development, 81,* 929–944.

5. **Blue's Clues:** To see an episode of Blue's Clues, go to YouTube and watch the episode, "Blues Birthday Party" (about 12 minutes long).

6. **Affective forecasting:** For a short review of research on affective forecasting, see Wilson, T., & Gilbert, D. (2005). Affective forecasting: Knowing what to want. *Current Directions in Psychological Science, 14,* 131–134.

7. **It's not the thought that counts:** Jeff Galak's research, and the source of my quotations from him, can be found in Galak, J., Givi, J., & Williams, E. F. (2016). Why certain gifts are great to give but not to get: A framework for understanding errors in gift giving. *Current Directions in Psychological Science, 25*, 380–385.
   (Italics added in the one Galak quote.)

8. **Desirable difficulties:** See Bjork, J. (2018). Being suspicious of the sense of ease and undeterred by the sense of difficulty: Looking back at Schmidt and Bjork (1992). *Perspectives on Psychological Science, 13*, 146–148.

9. **Studying by underlining as you read:** Simply underlining as you read something the first time doesn't help much. But, there are ways to use underlining as an effective study strategy. See Miyatsu, T., Nguyen, K., & McDaniel, M. (2018). Five popular study strategies: Their pitfalls and optimal implementations. *Perspectives on Psychological Science, 13*, 390–407.

10. **Blurry print and handwritten materials aid learning:** See Rosner, T. M., Davis, H., & Milliken, B. (2015). Perceptual blurring and recognition memory: A desirable difficulty effect revealed. *Acta Psychologica, 160*, 11–12. Also, Diemand-Yauman, C., Oppenheimer, D. M., & Vaughan, E. B. (2011). Fortune favors the bold (and the italicized): Effects of disfluency on educational outcomes. *Cognition, 118*, 114–118.

11. **Mindsets:** A good short overview of Carole Dweck, her mindsets research, and its history is Dweck, C. (2017). The journey to children's mindsets—and beyond. *Child Development Perspectives, 11*, 139–144. A longer, still-readable book-length treatment is her book, Dweck, C. (2006). *Mindset: The new psychology of success.* New York, NY: Random House.

Chpater 14

1. **Stories we live by:** Dan MacAdams's account of the stories and story–schemes that help us craft our sense of selves is presented nicely in MacAdams, D. (1993). *The stories we live by: Personal myths and the making of the self.* New York, NY: Guilford Press.

2. *David Copperfield: David Copperfield* by Charles Dickens was first serialized May 1849-November 1850. Published in book form 1850 by Bradbury & Evans, London. Fulll title of the book: *The Personal History, Adventures, Eperience and Observation of David Copperfield the Younger of Blunderstone Rookery.*

3. **Narrative everywhere:** Jerome Bruner famously insisted that humans have and incessantly use a narrative way of understanding their social worlds. See Bruner, J. (1986). *Actual minds, possible worlds.* Cambridge, MA: Harvard University Press.

4. **Understanding and misunderstanding emotions:** William James covers human emotions (along with perception, cognition, instincts, and consciousness) in Volume 2 of his 1890 *The Principles of Psychology* (New York, NY: Holt).

5. **Emotional faces:** Paul Ekman (also cited for research on lying in Chapter 2) conducted seminal research in the 1970s on the categorization of facial expressions into emotion categories (like, fear, anger, surprise). From this, he claimed that

emotion recognition was innate, direct, and universal across peoples in widely different cultures. Contemporary research shows, instead, that emotion recognition is not universal, and that reading the presence and nature of mental causes of emotions varies across societies. A good short overview of the issues and data is in Gendron, M., Crivelli, C., & Barrett, L. F. (2018). Universality reconsidered: Diversity in making meaning of facial expressions, *Current Directions in Psychological Science, 27*, 211–219. Ekman's FACS (Facial Action Coding System) remains a valuable and widely used tool to identify and code facial expressions according to their underlying use of facial muscles.

6. **Cognitive behavioral therapy (CBT):** CBT is a form of psychological therapy that helps clients with mood disorders, depression, and emotional anxiety by focusing on changing their distorted thinking. An early proponent was Aaron Beck, who created the widely used Beck Depression Inventory to diagnose and help psychologists treat depression. An easily digested description of the approach appears in the first chapters of Burns, D. (1980). *Feeling good: The new mood therapy.* New York, NY: Plume, 1980.

7. **Magic:** A good, short description of the psychological workings of magic is provided in Kuhn, G., Amlani, A., & Rensink, R. (2008). Towards a science of magic. *Trends in Cognitive Sciences, 12*, 349–354.

8. **Overestimating what we know, a community of minds:** See Sloman, S., & Fernbach, P. (2017). *The knowledge illusion: Why we never think alone.* London, England: Penguin.

9. **We all adopt a fundamental framework:** Quoted from Towles, A. (2016). *A gentleman in Moscow.* New York, NY: Barnes & Noble, p. 146.

Index